MORE WAYS TO WIN

By the same authors

HOW TO BE A WINNER

MORE WAYS TO WIN

How to be Happy and Successful in Life

Nick Thornely and Dan Lees

MERCURY

First published in Great Britain 1991
by Mercury Books

This edition reprinted 1998 by
Management Books 2000 Ltd,
Cowcombe House, Cowcombe Hill, Chalford,
Gloucestershire GL6 8HP
Tel: 01285-760722. Fax: 01285 760708
e-mail: MB2000@compuserve.com

Printed and bound in Great Britain by
Biddles Ltd, Guildford and King's Lynn

British Library Cataloguing in Publication Data is available

ISBN 1–85252–054–X

CONTENTS

Winners begin planning early

ACKNOWLEDGEMENTS

Jeffrey Archer, Dan Asterley, Mike Baker, Chris Bayliss, Steve Berry, Ken Bradford, John Bradley, Robin Breet, Tony Bryan, Chris Capron, John Chambers, Shirley Conran, R. Hon. John Cope MP, Tony Coward, David Cox, Anthony Coxhill, John Critchley, John Crook, Peter Dalton, Alec Davidson, John Davies, John Durston, Graham Edge, John Ford, Henry Foster, Ian Fox, Alistair Graham, Peter Granzow, Michael Green, Richard Halsall, Roy Hammond, Rhys Hedges, George Henderson, Lindsey Henniker-Heaton, John Hollingdale, Cyril Hollingworth, Pat Jameson, Vaughan Kelland, John Knox, Ian Lawrie, Mike Leece, Steve Lees, Ray Lewis, Iain Lindsay, Cliff Lovell, Jimmy Lowe, Peter Lutman, Michael Maberley, Paul Manning, Geoffrey Marshall, Richard Masterman, Muir Moffatt, David Monks, Bob Montgomery, Peter Morgan, Peter Mount, John Neill, Simon and Celia Preston, Nigel Reece, Nigel Renolds, Peter Robinson, Bob Sambrook, David Saunders, Jeff Seaward, Anita Sinclair, Tim Stanley, Geoffrey Stocks, Clement Stone, Derek Sturgess, Clive Swinnerton, Ann Thornely, Anthony Thornely, Ruth Thornely, Alan Tuffin, Karen Tully, Andrew Wall, Peter Walker, Brian Ward Lilley, Val Waterhouse, Martyn Wylie, Vivian Yuill.

1

WINNING IS SEXY

Winning is sexy, winning is fun – in fact winning is one of the most important things in life, so it's just as well that life is not a race or any other sort of sporting contest and that, instead of a few people running away with all the prizes and turning the rest of us into losers, there are thousands of ways to win and almost anyone can be a winner.

Of course it's great to win in obvious ways and there can't be much to beat gaining an Olympic Medal, becoming the heavy-weight boxing champion or winning an Oscar.

Making your first million must be quite a thrill too, as must being made boss of your firm or becoming Prime Minister but, as we pointed out in *How to be a Winner*, while there aren't enough of these super wins to go around, there are a lot of smaller victories to be won and even small wins can help us get the winning habit.

One thing we discovered while considering winning and winners in some detail was that some people who seem to be obvious winners are in fact hardly winners at all, because they confine their victories to a very limited sphere. These are the obsessed, the men and women who sacrifice everything to achieve one burning ambition and, having achieved it, discover that they are losers in almost every other respect.

The film star whose love life is a mess, the tycoon whose children are drop-outs or drug addicts – these losing winners are stereotype gossip-column fodder – but in most cases we don't have to look much further than our own neighbourhood or even our own families to find an example of a compulsive winner who has lost out on a lot of the good things in life. Of course, this doesn't mean that ambition is wrong or that it is wrong to want the best possible material conditions for ourselves and our families. In fact, real winners usually find that they achieve material success as a bonus, mainly because they are excellent choices for top jobs as well as being ideally suited to running their own businesses. At the same time, those compulsive winners who fail to develop as complete persons frequently become 'hatchet men', often attaining fairly senior positions, especially in large companies, but without reaching the top job they were aiming for, a situation which they of course find particularly galling.

One man who had retired after becoming a top executive with an international company confessed rather ruefully that he got a kick out of being nicknamed 'the Bastard' but thought that, had he been closer to the sort of winner we described in *How to be a Winner*, he might well have made it to the very top.

So, who are these 'real winners', how do we recognise them and, more important, how do we get to be winners ourselves?

WHAT MAKES A REAL WINNER?

While there are innumerable ways in which to become a winner, the best short definition of a winner we can come up with is someone who is 'happy in his or her skin'. These sorts of people can be dukes or dustmen, debs or dressmakers and we can usually spot them at a glance because they have presence, they command respect and they usually appear to be enjoying life a great deal more than most of the folk around them.

Enjoyment is a key factor in winning and helps to maintain the winning aura of habitual winners that makes them go on winning and endows them with a seemingly magical quality which is a great deal easier to recognise than to define.

The fact is that real winning is holistic and, in the sense that holistic medicine aims to treat the whole body, holistic winning involves winning in every aspect of life, which means that a genuine winner should not only have a healthy mind in a healthy body but a healthy, happy and contented mind in a healthy, happy and contented body.

HOLISTIC WINNING

Holistic winning, then, means winning right across the board rather than confining our wins to one or two specific victories to the exclusion of everything else. The whole person should win and almost always does so in such a way that other people win too.

Holistic winning involves another interesting concept in that it carries with it the idea that the whole is greater than the sum of its parts and in this particular case many small wins add up to something much more important than one would expect the accumulation to achieve.

Holistic winners of this sort are often seen as 'Fortune's favourites' or as men and women who 'have everything', the implication being that their being such obvious winners in all respects is a matter of luck, whereas in reality it is usually due to their being able to make the most of whatever possessions and talents they have. In this connection, as we pointed out, it isn't a lot of use being born with a silver spoon in your mouth if you can't find the plate.

WINNING LUCK

We don't deny the existence of luck – as we shall see, we are all of us extremely fortunate – but, given that there are so many ways in which to win, it was impossible to discuss them all in *How to be a Winner*. One way we didn't go into at length was luck.

We did talk about inherited and environmental advantages and argued that while it would be foolish to contest the fact that some people were born more beautiful, more intelligent or into richer or happier homes than others, there were sometimes ways in which such apparent advantages cancelled themselves out.

At the same time, apparent disadvantages sometimes brought their own compensations so that, say, a person with a speech impediment might, in struggling to overcome it, develop the skills needed to become a politician or a TV star.

However, we did admit that, even though its effects might not always be as expected and even though its adverse effects could often be minimised, there was a basic luck factor in that it was usually preferable to be born with reasonably good looks and to spend one's formative years in a loving, stable environment with the basic necessities of food, warmth and shelter at hand.

WINNING GREEN

Another sort of luck is the sort connected with windfalls, football-pool wins and pure happenstance and which ranges from monster chunks of good fortune to minor but enjoyable serendipities.

Curiously, we were the beneficiaries of one of these pieces of good luck ourselves as, no sooner had we nailed our colours to the mast, than we discovered that they embodied a fashionable hint of green and that our holistic view of winning – in which personal advancement and material gain were no longer the sole criteria of a successful life – was in tune with what many people had begun to see as a possibly less selfish decade than the 'Me! Me!' Eighties.

WINNERS ARE LUCKY

Winners are always being told how lucky they are, even though they are probably no more fortunate or unfortunate than anyone else. The thing is that winners do, by and large, have an optimistic view of the world, which means that they expect to be lucky, ensuring that when a stroke of good fortune comes along they recognise it and make full use of it.

That's why, having found our ideas on winning to be very much in tune with the spirit of the Nineties, we decided to follow up this winning streak by suggesting some *More Ways to Win*.

Tips from the Top

The better you prepare, the luckier you get.

If a book is worth reading – it's worth buying.

Sell your good qualities and don't dwell on your bad ones.

2

WINNERS ARE
THE GREATEST

Winners are wonderful – in fact, we are all wonderful, but winners know they are not only walking miracles but are also among the luckiest creatures in the universe.

Mind you, we may not feel particularly miraculous or lucky at the moment; perhaps we are even feeling a bit down, but as the lawyers say – usually as they are getting ready to stiff somebody – let's look at the facts.

It may be difficult to believe, but even the bleary-eyed, furry-tongued apparition that occasionally stares back at us from our shaving or make-up mirror is one of nature's genuine miracles and a lucky one to boot. For instance, just one drop of the red stuff that, on a bad day, makes our eyes look like urban road maps, contains some five million red blood cells.

On a better day, it's perhaps easier to accept that these are only a fraction of the 30 billion cells in our bodies, each one of which is a sophisticated chemical complex in its own right, a protein factory complete with power station, storage facilities and coded instructions for use.

Bleary or not, the eye peering out from our mirror contains 120 million rods and cones, capable of receiving millions of impulses during every second of our waking lives to join the millions of other impulses travelling along our nerve fibres to the brain for evaluation and analysis at some 200mph.

A miracle? Of course! We are all miraculous creatures and the first step towards becoming a winner is to realise it. 'Oh! What a piece of work is Man', said Shakespeare, meaning not only the great thinkers, famous soldiers, wealthy aristocrats, powerful magnates and so on but you, me and, for that matter, the cast of *Neighbours*.

Pretty impressive – even if most of us did know it all the time – but where does luck come in?

LUCKY ME, LUCKY YOU, LUCKY US

With a few desperately unfortunate exceptions, most of us would agree that being alive is a desirable state in itself so it's worthwhile considering how lucky we are to be here.

First, if we are to believe the latest thinking, some 15 million years ago there was the 'Big Bang' – itself perhaps merely a beat in the heart of Creation – which blasted out from an incredibly compressed starting point all the material which goes to make up the universe, including you and me. This eventually became millions of galaxies, including our own which contains around 100,000 million stars of which our sun is one.

Feeling lucky to be here? You should, because even though it is odds on that there is other intelligent life somewhere in the universe a lot of dust and gas just happened to be at the correct distance from the sun to make possible the creation of life in the form that would eventually lead to *you*.

If you are still not convinced, check out the odds against your ancestors surviving long enough to reproduce, in spite of hiccups like the Black Death and World Wars I and II,

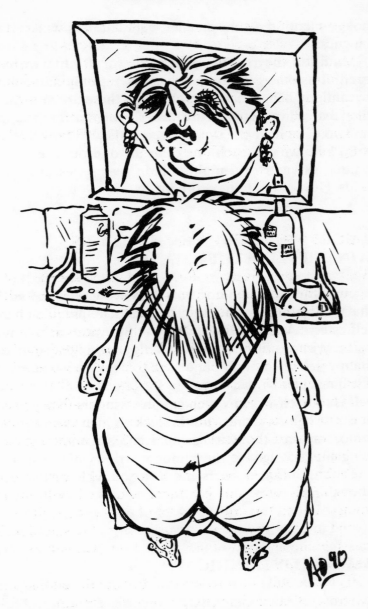

We are all miraculous creatures

not to mention all the smaller wars and less widespread plagues.

Mind you, the most impressive thing of all is that we have each of us emerged and survived as not only miraculous but unique beings because, although there are now more than five billion of us, we are all different and, for instance, no two of us have the same fingerprints.

So here we are, each one of us a wondrous creature, a unique survivor of a multi-million-year series of adventures. How miraculous – and lucky – can you get?

WINNERS LIKE THEMSELVES

It's worthwhile reminding ourselves every now and again that we are unique and special because it helps build up our self-esteem. Winners are always keenly aware of their own value. Winners like themselves – it's another way of being 'happy in one's skin' and one of the most valuable attributes of a winner.

It is this self-worth which enables winners to develop a personal comfort zone – a skin thick enough to provide an armour against the world's slings and arrows, often enabling them to ignore the minor worries which seem so important to non-winners and to get on with the business of winning.

BEWARE OF HANDICAPPERS

The trouble is that many of us have our self-esteem deliberately eroded by parents, siblings, classmates, teachers, employers and others, many of whom were themselves losers and, as such, assumed that losers would be easier to control than individuals aware of their own worth. Unfortunately, the low self-esteem imposed by such people is reinforced by the media which present us with a world populated by the rich, the famous, the powerful, the beautiful – and the rest of us.

By implication the gilded ones – including 'personentities' famous only for being famous – are winners, leaving the rest of us not only losers but losers who should be prepared to acknowledge their losing status.

In fact, for this system to work the losers must recognise their inferior status and be resigned to it, otherwise they might start checking on designs for state-of-the-art tumbrils and guillotines. This doesn't usually happen except in the case of ruthless rulers of poverty-stricken empires who are suddenly seen to have too many clothes. Instead whole industries spring up aimed at persuading losers to live vicariously through magazines, books, films and so on, detailing the luxurious lifestyles of the perceived winners.

Sociologists have even identified a tendency to defuse any envy on the part of losers by describing the terrible stress which fame and fortune bring in their train. This form of stress – which apparently strikes exclusively at those who have no financial worries and whose living and travel arrangements are rendered trouble-free by a band of retainers – is represented as being much worse than that suffered by ordinary mortals trying to bring up a family on a low salary or a state allowance and it would be funny, were it not for the fact that they are precisely the ones who are expected to sympathise with those who suffer from the stress caused by money and fame.

WINNERS ASK QUESTIONS

Winners are by no means immune to the persuasion that aims to enlist sympathy for the rich and famous but – and it's a big but – just when winners feel their eyes clouding over at the plight of some multi-millionaire slob, they tend to pull up sharp and ask themselves: 'Why the hell should I feel sorry for him when there are so many more urgent calls on my sympathy?'

Winners ask questions about everything, even if most of the time they are questioning themselves. 'Why should I do this? Why are people trying to make me think that? Who is going to benefit?'

Winners take care not to become paranoid – in fact being a winner protects them from thinking that everyone is against them – but they know that in the real world they can't afford to be naive and tend, for example, to read at least two newspapers, preferably presenting diametrically opposed views.

POSITIVE WINNING

We'll be looking at assertiveness which is a winning quality and comparing it with aggression which is usually a losing one but, for the moment, all we need to note is that assertiveness, if it is not to lead to our falling flat on our face, has to be firmly based on the confidence that comes from self-esteem. It is incredibly difficult to persuade people to value us highly if we ourselves are not convinced of our own worth.

This is why reminding ourselves that we are each of us a miracle is so important, especially when we begin life afresh at the start of each new day. The Victorians considered that a good breakfast was vital because to them it was not only nourishment but a reminder that, in an age when even relatively wealthy people could be beggared overnight, they still had plenty of food on the table. Today we need a different sort of reassurance but we still need to be convinced of our own worth before we start the day.

COPING WITH SELF-DOUBT

Most of us feel a touch of self-doubt every now and again – we'd be impossible to live with otherwise – but this is a long way from the low self-esteem from which many people suffer and which prevents them from becoming real winners.

Some women seem especially prone to low self-esteem – in many cases due to male brain-washing from a very early age, but it's heartening to note that in this particular, as in many others, women are creatures of Goldilocks extremes and that the many women who know their own value are shining examples of winners who hold themselves well, walk well, talk well and make the world a better place for themselves and those around them.

Permanent lack of self-esteem, as opposed to an occasional fit of the blues, is one thing that makes it virtually impossible to be a winner; in fact self-worth and winning make up a chicken-and-egg situation because while each win helps to bolster our self-esteem, boosting our self-esteem helps us win.

This being the case it's fortunate that, as we stressed in *How to be a Winner*, all of us can be winners and, if need be, we can start with small wins and build up on them as our self-esteem increases.

HOW MUCH ARE YOU WORTH?

There's an old story about the chap who went to a psychiatrist to get help with what he thought was his inferiority complex only to be told, 'I'm terribly sorry but you really *are* inferior'. So *are* some people really worth less than others?

Curiously, many of us who suffer from low self-esteem would be hard pressed to come up with genuine evidence of our inferiority but, even so, it would be fatuous to claim that we are all equal in every respect. Obviously, some of us are taller, stronger, prettier, brainier and so on than others, just as some of us are born into wealthy families and some into poor ones.

Self-esteem is largely a matter of punching our weight and making the most of what we have. We are all different but we are all miracles and, far from making us inferior, our differences make us unique so that there is a case for stressing those things about ourselves which set us apart from other people and help us to become winners.

Even physical attributes which might be seen as drawbacks can sometimes be turned into advantages; for example, there are fat comedians – and for that matter comediennes – who base whole careers on being overweight. Mind you, you don't have to be a giant or a dwarf to make your appearance an integral part of your personality and a relatively minor physical characteristic like flaming red hair which makes some people's lives hell can be a boon to others.

It's not easy to assess the value we put on ourselves partly because it often varies from day to day – but it's easy enough in general terms to find out whether our self-esteem is high or low.

HOW DO YOU VALUE YOURSELF IN RELATION TO OTHER PEOPLE?

Give yourself a mark on a scale of one to ten to indicate how clever you think you are. Assess in the same way how good-looking, attractive, efficient, likeable, fit, coopera-tive, assertive, etc. you think you are.

Now get your partner or an acquaintance to answer the same questions about you. If you can persuade them to answer the same set of questions about themselves it will help to ensure that they take the thing seriously. This is a straightforward simple quiz with no trick questions and if you consistently score under five the chances are that your self-esteem is too low.

If this is the case, what can be done about it? First of all you have to admit that like all human beings you are a pretty wonderful piece of machinery. Then look at any scores that were particularly low and decide what, if any-thing, can be done to improve them. Don't worry too much at this stage about the overall score because in the case of self-worth anything you do to improve your score in one field will automatically increase your score in most of the others.

Looks and fitness are important here so you could try following the precepts of *The Champagne Fitness Book* to help you improve them. Here, as in all winning, enjoyment is the keynote and the aim is to avoid boring diets or too much effort. Eat less and drink less but make both your food and drink more exciting and you'll find that, while the cost remains about the same, you will get the same or more satisfaction from what you eat and drink and will lose weight at the same time. Getting your weight right – and this includes putting on weight if that's what you need – will help you become more active, which in turn should make you better looking, sexier, more efficient and almost certainly wealthier. In other words, it's an ideal demonstration of holistic winning in that each win on the fitness front leads to more wins. The knock-on effect of all these wins – together with the fact that they help us to get the winning habit – goes a long way towards making us winners.

Serious physical defects are tough to cope with and it's as well to remember that very few people are physically perfect in every respect and even fewer remain perfect for the whole of their lives. Once again, it's a matter of degree and it sometimes seems as if those with the greatest handicaps become winners by making a supreme effort to overcome them, while those with minor deficiencies use them as excuses to remain losers.

WOULD BARBRA STREISAND HAVE A NOSE JOB?

Minor physical imperfections can often be either disguised, or corrected medically, and anyone who is worried about such things to the extent that worry is spoiling their enjoyment of life should have a word with a doctor and, if their own doctor appears unsympathetic, see another. Doctors are only human and not all of them, for example, appreciate the fact that a mole can seem like a mountain if you are the one who has it. Making a feature – a gimmick almost – of a physical defect is another way of handling this but you need to be a winner to carry it off. We knew one chap who lost his hand in a Western Desert tank battle and who frequently made himself the centre of attention, especially in mixed company, by using his metal fingertip to tamp down his pipe tobacco.

Personality traits with which we are not satisfied and which lead to low self-worth can almost always be improved once they have been recognised and evaluated. Most of them can be cured by winning but this does not mean that, if you feel you are not a particularly valuable person, the only way you can rid yourself of this feeling is to win a Nobel Prize, although of course it might help.

A small win – even a very small win – can increase our feeling of self-worth which in turn will help us to secure more small wins, leading eventually to bigger wins and a pleasing level of self-esteem.

START THE WINNING WAY

Try getting up half an hour earlier than usual. This means that you are not being jerked around by a boss or a schedule and gets you off to a winning start.

Do a little exercise before you shower and use a few minutes to take special care of your appearance. Choose your best, appropriate outfit including perhaps a new tie, scarf or ear-rings. Give your teeth an extra polish and your shoes an extra shine. Make a minor extravagance count by putting on a favourite after-shave or perfume and you're ready to start the day as a winner.

Liking ourselves is the first step in building up a series of inter-connected comfort zones, the next one of which could be the zone we build up with a partner.

Tips from the Top

Life is a football game – 35 years each way. You may not last the distance or you may play extra time.

There is very little difference in people. But that little difference makes a big difference. The little difference is 'attitude'. The big difference is whether it's 'positive' or 'negative'.

Time is the one ingredient in which we all have equal shares – 24 hours in each day. How we use these hours makes the difference. And we don't know for how many days.

3

WINNING FOR TWO

Love is a perfect example of a game for two players in which there should be no losers. In fact, it's a splendid example of a holistic win because, in terms of happiness and much else, the whole is greater than the sum of the two parts.

Sometimes, however, it seems as if this sort of partnership win is easier to sustain for a few weeks than a few decades and many people find that the romantic 'forever' of their youth gets to seem less like a dream and more like a life sentence.

Of course, we are not talking here about the hellish marriages from which death or divorce provide the only release. When things are as bad as that we can only say that a hellish marriage – like a hellish job – is something to get out of very quickly. If you have a 'parachute' in the shape of a new partner, we hope for your sake that he or she will make yours a winning team. Mind you, we wouldn't presume to offer an opinion on such a personal subject at all were it not for the fact that marriages and long-term partnerships can usually be improved by both the partners becoming winners.

At the same time, being a member of a winning partnership not only makes us winners at home – itself an important part of holistic winning – but also helps make us winners in the outside world – and especially at work.

WHAT MAKES A WINNING PARTNERSHIP?

Many of us expect too much from our partnerships and, since we frequently expect nothing less than perfection as our due, it's little wonder that we are so often disappointed.

However, just as frequently, because we have no means of knowing what's waiting for us round the corner, we are likely to pitch some of our expectations too low so that we miss out on some of the potential win factors in our partnership.

A list of the elements people expect to find in a winning partnership would vary enormously according to their age and circumstances but it would be likely to include such desirable things as companionship, great sex, mutual assistance and a compatible sense of humour.

It would be less likely to include things like a verbal shorthand and body language amounting to a private communication system, or the reciprocal back-up which enables a member of the partnership to face the world as a member of a winning team, or the conviction that each of the partners would have at least one person on their side – no matter what they did.

GREAT EXPECTATIONS

Grade your own partnership in respect of the basic expectations we have mentioned. Get your partner to check your answers if this is feasible but remember to make allowances for the current state of your relationship.

Next, let's look at the things which we have been led to expect from a partnership and which we think ought to be ours as of right when we decide to 'live happily ever after' under whatever social arrangements.

GREAT SEX

We don't have the space, the inclination or even the experience to write a sex manual but there are plenty of good ones around and – unless you feel you already know all there is to know about the subject – it is well worth reading a couple and then consigning them to the back of the bookcase. After all, although it's useful to know how everything works, few people feel the need to consult their car manual every time they set off for a drive.

However, winning in bed is important. For one thing it is a vital part of winning in the home and for another it illustrates, perhaps more than any other form of winning, the precept that in order to win you don't have to make someone else a loser and that, on the contrary, the way to become a winner is to make certain that the other person wins too. It is also a good example of holistic winning in that the total satisfaction is greater than the sum of the two parts.

Good manners, consideration and respect, together with a hint of humour, are more important than technique, while communication – especially when it develops into an exclusive 'language' – can be the most important thing of all. Above all, sex should be enjoyable for both parties. In sex, as in everything else, real winners assume they – and their partners – are going to win. There is nothing big-headed about this assumption which amounts merely to a mutual anticipation that all is going to go well.

If things don't go as well as they might – and winners are not exempt from headaches or drinking to much – then real winners have the self-confidence to say something like, 'Oh damn! Sorry – see you in the morning', rather than put in a panic call to the nearest marriage guidance counsellor.

In fact, while a good sex-life helps make people winners, being a winner is virtually a guarantee of good sex.

When you're a winner, no one has to lose

WHAT HAPPENED TO THE GOOD COMPANION?

If your parents have had a good marriage and you are enjoying a good relationship yourselves it is often difficult to envisage the barren waste in which some couples spend their lives. Even a visit to them isn't enough to provide much insight as both parties will usually be on their best behaviour. Only an extended stay will reveal that the couple are not a couple at all but merely two people who, in spite of the fact that they no longer even like each other, have agreed to go on sharing the same house or apartment.

The trouble is that it is all too easy for couples to fall into losing habits, without realising what is happening. Once a relationship has soured, it needs a conscious effort on the part of at least one of the partners to put it back on a winning course.

The sort of people we are talking about here rarely speak to each other except perhaps to indulge in verbal sniping and in such a situation the first question to ask ourselves, as potential winners, is, 'Could I – Heaven forbid – be at least partially to blame for this state of affairs?'

Ask yourself, for example, if you have behaved like less of a total winner than you might have done. Have you perhaps been too busy trying to win at work to maintain the home base – the comfort zone – that would help make you a winner in the workplace?

If the answer is even a half-hearted 'maybe' it could be time to make some changes, but don't try to change everything overnight. For one thing, if you do, your partner will be convinced that you have been up to no good!

Perhaps the best thing to do – and it could be the finest thing that could happen – is to explain to your partner that you intend to try out something you've read in a book – this one – which the authors claim could help make you a winner in the workplace.

Obviously, this would help make your partnership better off financially, so this is a point you could make fairly strongly, appealing to the enlightened self-interest which is part and parcel of the winning game.

This means that once you begin putting into practice some of the things we mentioned in Chapter 1 – like dressing better, keeping fitter, giving yourself time in the mornings and so on – your partner is at least going to understand what is going on rather than suspecting you are 'up to no good'.

The next step is to convert your partner into a team member who is actively helping to make your partnership a winning one.

A WINNING PARTNERSHIP

Building up a winning 'us against the world' partnership takes time but at least, once you have mentioned the winning concept, you have opened up a dialogue, which is vital, and you could be well on the way to finding out what it would take to make your partner a winner. At the same time, by making yourself a winner, you provide your part-ner – naturally without spelling it out – with both an example and an incentive.

Say, for example, that over the years you have become something of a careless slob. Now, as part of your cam-paign to become a winner, you could smarten yourself up and attempt to look better. It's odds on that if they too have let themselves go a bit they are going to follow your lead, just as, if you open up a conversation on a topic of real interest to your partners, you stand a good chance of getting a reaction. This may be simplistic but it is amazing how many people find it difficult to ask their partners, 'What sort of day did you have?' or, 'Shall we have a cup of coffee or would you rather have a gin and tonic?'

OPENING UP COMMUNICATION

Provided there are no distractions, it's difficult to have a drink together without exchanging at least a few words, so don't put the television on if it is off, and, if it's already on, ask if it is okay to switch if off or try to have your drink in a room without a TV set.

PRACTISING PARTNER-SPEAK

We will be coming across a great many winning words later on and a lot of them are applicable right across the board. The partnership words like 'we' and 'us' are a case in point. They are two words which can turn any losing argument into a winners' discussion because they are capable of turning two people into a partnership in spite of themselves. Try writing down a few lines of dialogue – half a dozen will do – in which you and your partner are discussing, say, money.

Do let's say 'money' in fact because it is one of the things many couples argue about most. Make it simple, make it realistic and, if you can reproduce an actual argument you have had recently, so much the better.

Use exclusively the 'I' and 'you' mode throughout and,

once you have written it to your satisfaction, read the scene into a tape recorder playing both voices yourself where appropriate.

You could finish up with something like, 'Just look at this! Have you seen this bank statement? You've been spending a fortune on clothes lately and I'm not putting up with it. You're going to have to cut down. You seem to think I'm made of money!'

Now translate what you have written into 'partner-speak', beginning by using the 'we' and 'us' mode. The first thing you'll notice is that it is difficult to substitute the words without changing the sentence.

Even if you start off with 'Have you seen this bank statement?', as soon as you switch modes the next few sentences turn into something like, 'We seem to have been spending far too much money on clothes recently. I think we'd better cut down for a while, don't you? After all, we're not made of money, are we?' Now read the new version into the tape recorder. Already it is more difficult to say angrily and although it is not yet perfect 'partner-speak', the implications of the changes are enormous. Already you and I have become a team – 'we' – and the implication is that our finances are a joint purse, the spending of which is a matter for discussion.

Other changes suggest themselves as a result of this change in attitude brought about by substituting team words for divisive words. For example, since we have a joint purse, the sentence 'after all we're not made of money, are we?' isn't total team-speak. Try substituting, 'Things should be better in a couple of months when we'll have a bit more money.' Try making similar changes in your original argument and see how it becomes a discussion. Then – if you have been imagining yourself as Voice A – play the recording of your argument again, but this time imagine that you are Voice B. This can be quite revealing. Then do the same thing with your 'discussion' on the same topic and decide which sounds more like a winning team at work.

Later, when your partner has become involved in the winning effort, you could try it with both of you playing the scene, if only to prove that neither of you is manipulating the other in any bad sense. What you are doing is manipulating your communications to your mutual advantage. In other words – both of you are winning.

– OR FOR WORSE

Help in times of need or sickness comes fairly high on the list of what most people expect from a partnership and surprisingly these expectations are sometimes realised even when the rest of the partnership has crumbled. In many cases adversity and especially illness bring out hidden resources in a partner.

If you are not getting all the help you need from your partner perhaps you aren't making it obvious that you really need it or perhaps you are taking too much for granted. It is too much to expect, say, round-the-clock nursing as a matter of course, but winners will get it, largely because they have invested – without thinking of it in that way – a great deal of goodwill, not to mention love, work, money and the rest, in the partnership bank.

In the same way a winner who suffers career reverses will not only have a shoulder to cry on but often financial help from his or her partner. This in fact is something that winning partnerships cater for as part of their Worst Possible Scenario plan and, as with help in times of sickness, the general rule is that the more you invest the more you are able to count on. Mind you, there are rogue partners and masochistic partners who are exceptions to this rule but winners should not have been naive enough to fall for the former or sufficiently sadistic to encourage the latter.

Winners invest in their partnerships. They also try to keep their partnerships as equal as possible even to the extent of sharing the leadership role. There's an old joke about the man who said he took all the big decisions in his household, like determining their attitude on foreign policy or the International Monetary Fund, while his wife made all the smaller ones like where they were going to live and what sort of car they would buy. Winning partners don't work quite like that but winners do know that their partners have different fields of expertise which can be useful to the partnership.

REAL STROKES FOR CLOSE FOLKS

People like to be complimented, which makes 'stroking' an important part of a winner's armoury. Partners not only respond well to verbal stroking but usually enjoy an affectionate hug into the bargain. Most men know, for instance, that women who cook for a partner like to be told that a particular meal was great, especially if they get a bit of a cuddle to go with the compliment, but only winning women seem to realise that their tough, hard breadwinner likes to be reassured every now and then in much the same way.

Even these days, women who have a career still take most of the responsibility for looking after the home and children. Winning partners, as well as helping, should be lavish in praise and appreciation. Burning resentment in one partner and lack of understanding in the other can destroy what might have been a winning team.

FUNNY – NOT FUNNY?

Humour is important in winning partnerships but it has to be mutual. Humour which makes the other person the target of hurtful jokes is definitely not winning humour.

This is not to say that close partners can't indulge in some fairly hard-hitting verbal battles, especially when they are evenly matched. Long-time partners can often communicate the fact that they have had enough or that things are becoming dangerously close to serious merely by altering their tone of voice, but if partners can't manage this it could be an idea to have a word like the ones which ended ritual playground battles. Do kids still say 'pax', for example, when bloodshed begins to seem inevitable?

A cheap laugh at your partner's expense, especially if you are with a group of friends, can be particularly hurtful and lead to the 'you're always trying to put me down in front of people' complaint. Winners don't belittle their partners – they build them up and so help create a winning partnership.

Tips from the Top

If relationships are right, all other problems are easy to resolve.

Never be afraid to say you're sorry.

No problem is usually two problems. Firstly, there usually is a problem and secondly, the person in charge doesn't know it!

4

HOW TO WIN AT HOME

As any footballer will confirm, if you can't win at home you're unlikely to win away because home is where your fans are, home is the place you are used to and home is where you are most likely to be a hero.

Your home should also be a comfort zone, a base from which you set out to conquer the world, which means that next to self-esteem, and a winning partnership, your home may well be the most important factor in becoming an overall or holistic winner.

Even if you now live on your own, the influence of your family home lives on and the place you now occupy should be a base, a retreat and a potential comfort zone. Those of us whose early life was spent in what was, at best, a cold comfort zone often find that selective memory enables us to forget the worst aspects of it and to concentrate on the present.

For those who don't have even a few pleasant memories of childhood as a mental comfort zone to fall back on, especially if there is no partner to help us, building up a base becomes of prime importance.

Fortunately, landladies and neighbours may well become part of this surrogate home team, as may fellow members of a club or the regulars at a friendly local.

Obviously, the closer people are to you, the more help they are able to give you in becoming a winner and if you

A comfort zone

live with others they should be your most valued fans. If it sometimes seems as though they are your only fans this merely emphasises their importance.

There again, if the home fans turn against you, which can happen in life as in football, their hostility is more wounding than that of anyone else, which makes winning at home of paramount importance.

HOME DRAWS DON'T COUNT

Unfortunately, many people – perhaps even the majority – are not winners at home. They live in a state of armed truce with the rest of their family, broken by hostile acts, ranging from verbal sniping to outright physical violence, with every grade of unpleasantness in between. The trouble is that, while in cases where family life is totally impossible the answer though painful is fairly obvious, the more frequent cases in which home life is bearable, but only just, present a more difficult problem.

Usually the answer to an intolerable situation, either at home, in the workplace or elsewhere, is to try one's damnedest to put things right and if this proves impossible – to win with your feet and move.

With families things are often not quite bad enough to force us to make a break but still bad enough to make us feel that we must get out of the house. In fact sociologists have even identified a tendency among people who are not happy at home to escape to work.

ESCAPE TO A COMFORT ZONE

People who spend an inordinate amount of time at work often do so because they can't face the thought of going home. The work in question may not always be ideal but it does offer a comfort zone – perhaps an office where they can shut the door and be quiet, perhaps a place where they feel their efforts are appreciated and their status respected. However, escaping to work only serves to exacerbate the situation that the workaholic has left behind. The fact is that if you want to be a holistic winner you must be a winner at home and a home draw isn't good enough.

The worst thing is that while, as we have seen, self-worth is fundamental to winning, the people who share our home can slowly undermine our self-esteem and even cut it to ribbons, often without being aware of how much harm they are doing.

Sometimes a family's sniping criticisms or deprecating remarks aimed at one of its members can become a matter of habit, almost unconscious on the part of the perpetrators, and accepted as normal by the hapless victim. Sadly, even though masquerading as humour, this can be vicious and destructive and in the end it's not just the victim who loses but the whole family.

Family persecutors are often compensating for their inability to win elsewhere but this only makes things worse for the victims, many of whom spend half a lifetime of effort in school, on the sports' field or at work in a vain attempt to gain a word of praise from their parents. Frequently the only winning answer in cases like this is to move out and to make sure that when you set up your own home it is a genuine comfort zone where no one is subject to impossible stress in an attempt to make the others seem like winners.

As in all winning, the secret of the home win is to make sure that everyone ends up a winner.

A HOME WIN IS A WIN, IS A WIN

Fortunately a small win is as important at home as anywhere else – perhaps even more important than anywhere else – so let's begin winning at home.

We have already got off to a good start by realising that we are miraculous, unique and fortunate creatures. We have also made certain of some small but important wins on the home front by getting up a few minutes earlier than usual. This is primarily to avoid the feeling that the boss – or the diary – is already controlling our actions but, like most wins, it has a bonus or knock-on effect even if it only makes us less impatient when, say, the only bathroom is in use.

In fact those extra minutes can make the world of difference to our day and that of everyone in the house.

START THE DAY A WINNER

There's no real need to organise the family's start to the day with inflexible military precision – that way you'll only get mad if something upsets the time-table – but it makes sense to plan how best to use the extra time you have given yourself.

BE YOUR OWN VALET OR LADY'S MAID

These days very few of us have servants but it can be useful to make a list of the things we would ask them to do for us and then to see how we can do them ourselves.

Be your own valet

This, of course, is a counsel of perfection but, while few of us will ever become completely organised – or would want to – there is usually a case for considerable improvement. For example, before going to bed:

(1) Check that your outfit for the next day – suit, dress or whatever – is clean and pressed and hanging over the back of a chair or on an easily accessible hanger.

(2) Check that clean underclothes, tights, socks and so on are to hand.

(3) Clean shoes if appropriate.

(4) Lay out wallet, purse, money – especially change you are bound to need for bus fares, toll fees, etc. – hand-kerchief, credit cards, business cards, pen, diary, pocket calculator, season ticket, make-up bag – in short the bits and pieces you always carry with you – in a handy and regular place. Check that papers you will need are in your briefcase and make sure that your car keys are where they should be.

(5) If you are running out of toothpaste, now is the time to locate a new tube and to make sure that there's enough soap and that your hairbrush hasn't decided to go walkabout.

Add your own items to the list as appropriate.

For instance, one busy young career woman we know hangs up six complete outfits in her wardrobe every weekend – one for each working day the following week plus an extra in case of diasaster – together with a bag looped over each hanger containing clean underwear and claims it ensures a more relaxed start to her day without the desperate panic of, 'What shall I wear?'

PARTNERS AS VALETS

When one partner goes out to work while the other stays at home the home-based partner often does a lot to help the other get ready for work. Although things are gradually changing, this usually means that the wife helps her husband to get ready for work – or the mother her children – and the main thing to remember is that, whoever does it, this is an extremely important factor in helping the breadwinner to win bread and make the partnership – or the family unit – a winning one. It should never be taken for granted.

START THE DAY WARM UP

Even if you have not yet begun a formal exercise programme you could try a few leg-raises, sit-ups, press-ups or running on the spot, according to your age and present level of fitness. If you do only enough to make you feel slightly out of breath it's a help. Stand by an open window, wherever feasible, not only for the fresh air but to exercise eye muscles by focusing on objects more distant than books or TV sets. Then, unless you find it absolute torture, try running the cold water for a couple of seconds after your hot shower. It needn't even be icy cold at first – just cool enough to make the contrast invigorating. At some time during the bathroom routine, spend a few seconds grimacing into the mirror to exercise jaw and neck muscles.

TIMING TO WIN

Some of the time you spend on basic relaxation exercises could easily be made up by having your outfit and accessories for the day ready in advance. Eventually you might be able to persuade the rest of the family to adopt time-saving routines and some model scheduling, but it could take a few days to get used to the new morning routine. Allow an extra fifteen minutes on the first few mornings to be on the safe side.

Naturally, as a winner, you will have discussed your proposed change in routine with the rest of the family, especially your partner, being careful to explain how *they* will benefit as you become better organised. No need to mention what could easily be the most important benefit of all, namely the change for the better in your early-morning disposition – they'll notice that soon enough for themselves.

GOOD-MORNING WINNERS

Of course, it goes without saying that winners greet their families with a smile and a cheerful 'good morning' – so why do many families' mornings begin with grunts and groans?

It does not need to be like that. The new you – refreshed, invigorated and with time to spare – really does have a chance to greet the family and, who knows, after the first shock is over you may even get a half-hearted smile in return. Well, it's a start.

KICK THE HALO INTO TOUCH

Just before you meet the family – and the rest of the world – as a winner it could be a good time to remind yourself that winners aren't saints. We certainly have no aspirations in that direction. You don't really need an altruistic bone in your body to become a winner. Just believe that the best way to become a winner is by making the people around you feel like winners and you've cracked it. Naturally, if you can manage to make your family feel like winners you have brought off the double, but take it easy in case people think you have gone round the bend. For instance, as a winner you know that people love being stroked but, if you have been a lifelong curmudgeon, it wouldn't do to pay too many compliments to start with. Ration yourself at first to a couple of compliments a day and then increase the dose.

When it comes to winning the home is not only a splendid base but also a laboratory in which you can learn how to win with people by making them into a winning team.

MAKE YOUR CASTLE INTO A HOME

An Englishman's home is his castle, or so they say, and in spite of a certain amount of erosion and one or two breaches in the walls our homes are still largely free from physical interference from the outside. The trouble is that if your castle is a one-room flat or a house that feels like a nursery-rhyme shoe it sometimes seems as though it would need a great deal of imagination to turn it into a comfort zone.

Most of us need privacy occasionally and of course if you

Make your castle into a home

have enough rooms it is simple for everyone in the house to have his or her own space.

In a small house it is worth thinking about rationing privacy; two children sharing a room, for example, could have a certain amount of private time every day. Even in a small room a rearrangement of furniture or shelving could create private areas. In good weather it's worthwhile using the garden, if you have one, as an extra sitting room and dining room, the bonus being that the garden is easier to keep tidy than an inside room.

The English, even those with minuscule houses, have always thought that the parlour should be the parlour while the bedroom is a bedroom and nothing else; French people with a similar-sized house might see a small bedroom as being, in addition to sleeping quarters, a study, a library, a wine cellar, a studio, a workroom and so on. If they were short of space they certainly wouldn't leave one of their rooms empty for sixteen hours a day simply because the estate agent had designated it a 'bedroom'.

If everyone in the house has a room of their own you are fortunate as you can each have a private bed-sitting room, but not everyone has enough rooms and those of us living in cramped conditions have to use consideration and ingenuity to obtain private time. Men sometimes find a quiet visit to the pub, the garden shed or the allotment useful while one photographer we knew, who found himself sharing a small flat with a brother, a couple of colleagues and the appropriate number of girlfriends, used to retreat to the smallest room in the house every morning for half an hour of contemplation.

BAN BREAKFAST BUST UPS!

They used to say that you should never let the sun go down on your wrath, but while it's not a good move to go to bed seething with rage it is even worse to arrive at the breakfast table boiling over with anger. There's no really good time for rows but going to work after a row that has upset the whole family is far from a winning move and won't make anyone's day.

You could try being extra pleasant in the mornings or at least make a tacit agreement not to bring up any contentious subjects until evening.

MAKE A TV-BAN TREATY

Many families who are living in a state of open warfare, and even more who exist in a state of armed truce, use the TV set as a smoke screen and a weapon. They use it to render conversation impossible which means that no one can win.

Often no one is actually watching whatever is on and a little careful study of the programmes should make it possible to find a half-hour or so which could be made into an informal TV break. As any direct salesman will tell you, it's no good merely turning down the sound; you have to turn off the set if you want people to listen. Of course, the first few times you opt for deafening silence and that fearsome lack of hypnotic flicker you should try to have something interesting and advantageous to discuss, like a party or a holiday. Once the TV break has proved its usefulness in making the whole family winners it can be used to ventilate more contentious matters like daily chores or who gets to use the car.

The TV break could also be a good place to hand out praise and winning style criticisms on the lines of 'It's great, but perhaps you could . . .?'

WARM UP YOUR COLD COMFORT ZONE

Your home should be a comfort zone – a retreat for bruised egos, a power base, a castle, a nest, a womb and lots more besides; a real home in fact.

It should also be portable in that you ought to be able to take a lot of the comfort you derive from your home out into the world and especially into the workplace. Knowing that you have a supportive team at home, even if it is a team of one, makes all the difference to winning away.

The trouble is that some people – often, but not always men – who find it tough to win at work, think they can win at home by being bullies and tyrants. Such people – usually members of the Jobsworth clan, the born losers we met in *How to be a Winner* – are losers, because only losers would alienate their potential fans.

A comfort zone, not a cold comfort zone, is what winners should aim for because a winning home gives you a base from which you can conquer the world.

Tips from the Top

The truth often hurts feelings the most.

Don't take the first 'no' for a final answer.

God gave us one mouth and two ears – learn to use them in that ratio.

5

WINNING WITH CARS – AND THINGS

Leaving the house? Don't forget your comfort zone! After all, it's much more important than your umbrella – although your umbrella could well be part of it.

As we have seen, winners are 'happy in their skin' and have winning partnerships and winning families which make their homes into comfort zones, so that when they go out to face the world they are able to take a portable comfort zone with them.

A great deal of this comforting cocoon consists of the certainty that they are going out as part of a winning team with all that entails in the way of back-up, but there are a number of material things which can be used to strengthen this sort of comfort zone.

WINNING WITH CLOTHES – AND WITHOUT THEM

Old-fashioned mums used to insist that their children never left the house without clean underwear – in case they got knocked down – but winners tend to look on the bright side, so perhaps we should determine never to leave the house without being prepared to meet the love of our life or at the very least a head-hunter seeking to fill a dream job. Basic cleanliness and personal hygiene ought to go without saying, but so many losers lose simply because their fingernails are in deep mourning or their armpits smell of dead hedgehog that it's worthwhile stressing that *winners are clean*.

This doesn't mean that winners can't be sloppy dressers if that's the style that conveys their particular winning message.

For some winners, for instance, an elderly Savile Row suit or jacket provides a more effective sartorial comfort zone than the new equivalent from an expensive multiple tailor. In many cases comfort-zone clothing is the equivalent of a child's comfort blanket and wives who have got rid of their husband's favourite old fishing jacket are often astounded by the belated discovery that they have inadvertently chipped away a little of their husband's persona.

'*Kleider machen Leute*' say the Germans – clothes make the man – and so, to some extent they do, but this doesn't mean that we should all wear uniform. Winners dress to suit themselves and to convey the message they intend to convey – which usually means that they are appropriately dressed for the occasion. When it comes to clothing, as with much else, winners buy the best they can afford, and they know how to wear whatever they choose with the style and confidence which makes their clothes a tangible part of their comfort zone.

If you can't afford to dress expensively, buy one small accessory like a tie, a scarf or a pair of shoes which is the finest available. Winners are as childish as the next person and it's wonderful what confidence can be derived from the secret conviction that you are wearing a better tie than the boss. In much the same way a discreetly expensive perfume or aftershave need not break the bank but it does help provide that winning aura.

Winners are never afraid to enlist help when it's available and if your partner is frequently commended for fashion consciousness or dress sense it's worthwhile soliciting their opinion.

Winners never try to make other people losers so, if a member of the family asks you for an opinion on their outfit, 'Are you sure that's quite you? It doesn't really show off your small waist, good legs, etc., etc.' could be a winning reaction to something hideously unsuitable. Remember that folks like to be stroked so look for something worthy of a genuine compliment.

WINNING WITH CARS

Cars are a splendid example of the mobile comfort zone. They are private space and, especially when used for driving to work, can be an extension of the home comfort zone or even a replacement for it.

Here, the lone driver, who may well have chosen the décor and the furnishing of the car, also gets to choose the entertainment, the noise level, the temperature and the air circulation. In addition he or she is in charge of the vehicle which, traffic permitting, moves entirely at the whim of the driver.

Some psychologists believe the car to be a symbol of sexual potency but, whatever the truth of this, the car does place its driver in a position of power which makes it a good field in which to win.

Curiously enough, one winning decision might well be not to have a car at all and although most of us have been sold on the desirability, if not the inevitability, of car ownership it is often worth asking if it is really worthwhile – if only on financial grounds. City-dwellers, faced with horrendous parking bills, fines, clamping and tow trucks may well find the use of taxis for short journeys and car hire for longer trips a viable alternative. People who live in or close to smaller communities may also choose not to own a car, especially if they like a drink, but this still leaves plenty of people who either choose to or need to run their own vehicle.

CHOOSING A MOBILE COMFORT ZONE

Obviously the person who spends most time in the car should usually make the final decision on what to buy, but winners tend to let partners and family members have a voice. This not only helps to make them feel like members of a winning team but can provide useful input on special requirements like sports' gear stowage or boot space and accessibility for family shopping.

If money is no object that ought to be the end of it, apart from an absorbing study of catalogues, visits to car showrooms and test drives. However, even wealthy winners have a few more factors to consider, perhaps the most important being the comfort-zone factor, but by and large, if you have the cash and can spend it without depriving other team members of anything vital like food, buy whatever car you like, with one important proviso. If you find after a reasonable settling-down period that you hate the damn thing – get rid of it!

A car that is a worry isn't a mobile comfort zone so whether you are buying new or secondhand, buy a vehicle

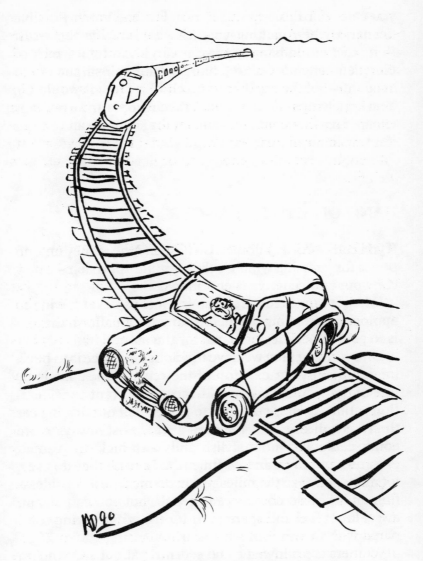

A car that's a worry isn't a mobile comfort zone

you can afford to buy and to run. Use the Worst Possible Scenario when making your choice. Imagine the worst thing that could happen to your car, like a total wreck or complete engine failure, and – taking insurance into account – ask yourself how much of a blow it would be. You are a winner if a few choice swear words and a perhaps cheaper replacement car would fit the situation and a loser if it would mean near bankruptcy.

BANG ON WITH A BANGER

If you can't afford or don't wish to spend the money on – no prizes for guessing which is the winning approach – a new car, your choice range is enormous.

When it comes to cars, winning means never having to apologise so, having decided what you can afford, the aim is to get the best deal you can for the money.

One winning ploy we have used once or twice is to buy a largish, quality car or a top-of-the-range vehicle made by one of the giants. Perhaps the most important consideration is that it's more difficult to knock hell out of a big car than a small one, but they are also almost always more comfortable and more stylish and, with luck, they could even turn out to be an investment. Of course they do use a lot more petrol so the mileage you do must be a consideration and they do cost more to repair, but you can buy an awful lot of fuel and spare parts for the initial saving compared with the price of a new car.

Winners are allowed to be eccentric about cars and an elderly Rolls Royce, for example, yields much more winning 'road cred' than a much younger run-of-the-mill vehicle with the same price tag.

Here again, winners seek advice when they need it so, unless you are a mechanic, it's worthwhile getting the AA or RAC to run the rule over your intended purchase.

Winning moves, once you get your new baby home, include a good clean inside and out. Empty and wash the ash trays, polish fascias and so on, as well as cleaning the carpets. Fit new mats and new covers to the foot pedals if they are worn and leave the windows open if possible to get rid of any lingering stale smells.

For a few pounds more you can often give an elderly car a heart transplant by investing in a new battery and spark plugs while, if the tyres are even slightly suspect, new ones will add as much to your image as a lover of quality cars as they will to your safety.

Winners have well-functioning and new-looking inertia reel seat belts and never force either themselves or others to struggle with shredded bits of frayed and twisted canvas. After all a winner's car is a comfort zone.

BE A WINNING PASSENGER

Remember, if you are riding as a passenger in someone else's car, especially if you are not a member of the driver's family or an intimate friend, that you are in someone's private space. This is perhaps why 'back-seat driving' is regarded as more of a crime than most forms of criticism. You are there by invitation of course but, none the less, to some extent you are an intruder and while the car provides an interesting modification to the rules about getting too close to people, there is often a lingering element of unease.

Winners behave in other people's cars – and in their own for that matter – as if they are in a well-furnished drawing room in which they are perhaps forced to share a fairly short sofa. Propinquity and the temporary suspension of the rules on physical closeness, as many couples have discovered, make the car an ideal ice-breaker, but while winners may take advantage of this happy circumstance they will be more aware than others that, while space limitation can be agreeable, space invasion as such can be harassment.

Winners who learn to appreciate cars as mobile comfort zones will realise why criticism of a driver's vehicle can sometimes be taken as a deadly insult. One adverse comment can lose a sale or ruin a relationship while a single pat on the bonnet can make you an instant winner.

Fortunately there is usually some pleasant remark you can make about most cars – even if it is only to comment on the low petrol consumption – which is just as well, since many drivers will have taken more care in choosing their vehicle than they did about choosing their partner.

We ourselves tend to go for the classic new or the classic old – cars of course – according to our current circumstances, but other winning approaches to the car question include a classless Mini if you live in town and do most of your driving there or an elderly Land Rover if you live an inch past the suburbs.

WINNING WITH MR NICE GUY

Getting up those few minutes earlier helps winners to leave a harmonious comfort zone behind them which makes them better able to cope with the frustrations of the road.

Even these frustrations are eased by leaving a few minutes earlier because the pressure is off and it can prove possible on occasions to take a slightly longer route to avoid the worst of the traffic.

However, no matter which route you take, this could well be the first time since getting up in the morning that you come up against members of the Jobsworth clan. This sad, widespread family is represented in most grades of society so the mobile Jobsworth is as likely to be driving a top-of-the-range BMW as a tiny banger with nodding dogs or fluffy dice in the rear window. Their only distinguishing feature on the road is their incredibly bad judgement, and even worse manners, which is their way of countering a lifetime of losing frustration.

A highly satisfying way of countering the motorised Jobsworth is to drive with impeccable manners and near super-human consideration, especially as winners employing these tactics often seem to finish up in front anyway.

WINNING WITH UMBRELLAS

If you choose not to have a car you can still take your comfort zone with you by riding a good motorcycle or a top-of-the-range push bike and, even when they decide to walk, winners may well carry the finest of umbrellas which adds winning panache to their appearance at relatively low cost. Again, a good-quality briefcase, if you need one at all, is another way of taking a little of your comfort zone to the workplace as well as being a useful announcement that your work is important to you. A briefcase, which should not be stuffed full – a spare set of underwear and toilet gear, especially if accompanied by a passport, is the only winning exception to this rule – provides a useful transition if you have driven into work from the comfort zone of your car to what you intend making the comfort zone of your workplace.

Tips from the Top

Never rest easy with success of today – prepare with Plan 'A' or Plan 'B' for tomorrow.

Assume nothing – if you do make assumptions, they will quickly bounce back and bite you on the bum.

I'm always nervous about people who tell me how busy they are.

6

WINNING WITH WORDS

Winners often give the impression that their winning is all done by magic and that their amazing ability to emerge triumphant from almost any situation is due to some innate and mysterious gift which other people do not possess.

In fact, winners *do* make use of magic words, magic phrases and even incantations but, even though such words sometimes appear to confer magic powers on their users, there is really nothing mysterious about them – apart from the mystery of language itself.

Language is the thing that sets us apart from most, if not all, of the rest of creation and it is one of the greatest single factors in helping us to become winners.

LANGUAGE AS COMFORT

Winners make use of the fact that language is an important part of people's comfort zones. The special words used by lovers, partners and families, the jargon used by professionals, thieves' cant, slang and even languages themselves are comfort-zone accentuators but they do tend to result in 'them and us' situations, as when the Greeks called foreigners 'barbarians' because their languages sounded like the noises made by sheep.

Winners know that learning even a few words of a language – however exclusive – can help prevent them being regarded as total outsiders. Language can help us win the object of our desires, language can make us into leaders of men; it can persuade, frighten, comfort, arouse, hurt or hypnotise. It is an extremely powerful tool for good or for evil but it is not the exclusive property of any one type of class or person and, while it is perfectly possible to be trained in its use, too much training can be self-defeating.

Simplicity is one of the keynotes of winning language and two of the most magical words in any tongue are among the simplest of all.

BASIC MAGIC

Two words – 'please' and 'thank you' – hold more power than most of us imagine. They are of more use than all the etiquette books ever written and more valuable than any number of tomes on man management. They are the basics of the winners' vocabulary and one of the marks of a losing relationship, a losing family or a losing firm is the neglect of these all important words. They are the basic currency of social and commercial exchanges and their importance can be determined from their place in foreign-language primers – usually immediately after the all-important 'My name is . . .'.

Like most currencies, words can be debased and falsified, so winners are careful to use even simple words like 'please' and 'thank you' with care – and sincerity. Winners, for example use 'please' not only in requests but when giving orders and instructions. They certainly do not fall

The basics of the winner's vocabulary

into the trap of thinking that being a boss means never having to say 'please' or 'thank you'.

Winners use 'thank you' frequently, in order to 'stroke' other people and they usually manage to make these words and the other small change of language into the equivalent of a 50-pound note. There's a world of difference between a curt 'thanks', for example, and the boss who makes a special trip to your office or work station just to say 'thank you'.

Winners go out of their way to say 'thank you' and this includes sending a memo or a note where appropriate. We know of several writers, for instance – including people like Jilly Cooper and James Herriot – whose habit of dashing off thank-you notes makes the recipients feel like winners themselves. The fact that the notes are a good winning move is a typical winners' spin-off.

'HELP!'

One very simple winning phrase is, 'Could you help me please?' which, whether you are asking for a loan of a million quid or directions to the nearest pub, contains a well-nigh irresistible stroking element of implied superiority. People like to help, especially when assistance either costs them nothing or makes sound business sense, which is why this phrase and variants like, 'I wonder if you could help me . . .?' are genuine winners.

ORDERS IS STILL ORDERS

For managers especially, basic communications winning has to include phrases like, 'Would you mind?' and variations like, 'I wonder if you'd mind?' rather than, 'Do such and such immediately or I'll boot your bottom out of the door.' It is just that it makes the recipient of the instructions happier to carry them out and helps them feel more a winner long after the whole business of giving and taking orders has been completed.

WINNING WORDS

Make your own list of winning words and phrases. Try to remember and note down occasions on which people have given you instructions in ways that have left you feeling (a) well-disposed towards them and happy to comply and (b) disgruntled rather than a winner. You could be surprised to discover how long the memory of how people spoke or wrote to you has lasted – a fact which emphasises how important winning words can be.

ACCENTUATE THE ACCENT

Regional accents are now almost universally acceptable and many winners make a feature of their distinctive speech, sometimes basing whole careers on that one characteristic. However, as the purpose of communication is to communicate, winners differentiate between interesting accents and sloppy unintelligible speech.

Winners frequently behave like linguistic chameleons, modifying their speech very slightly according to circumstances. This doesn't mean that they imitate other people but rather that they lean towards their speech habits and accents, which is a winning social and professional accomplishment.

Actors are often able to win with words, partly because of their ability to modify their accents and partly because they are taught to speak clearly, which enables them to project their voices through a babble of sound and to command attention – often a prerequisite of communication. Winners don't often need to shout. In fact one winning move is to speak softly so that people have to concentrate in order to hear but it is still necessary to get their attention in the first place.

KNICKERS

It's on the cards that, even if you were just flicking through this book, the heading at the top of this paragraph was one which drew your eyes and made you stop – even though it is a perfectly unremarkable and harmless word for an article of clothing. Its attention-grabbing quality is almost certainly due to its being completely out of context, a 'sore-thumb' syndrome which can be useful in all forms of communication.

There's an old story about an English lady who remonstrated with a donkey driver she saw hitting his charge with a stick. When asked why he didn't just speak to it, the driver replied that he would do just that – as soon as he had its attention.

Take a thought break and consider the way we could use words to attract attention. You probably won't often have to go as far as the chap we heard of who was living in France and was owed what, to him, was a large sum of money by a department of a huge London-based company, run by a man he knew fairly well. Over a period of months a number of letters, ranging from chatty to desperate, elicited no money – in fact not even a response – until our hero devised a letter beginning with the most flowery French salutation he could find and ending at the bottom of the page with the phrase which translates, 'Please be good enough to accept my most respectful and sincere good wishes etc.' Then, in the dead centre of the otherwise blank page he wrote in capitals:

WHY DON'T YOU ANSWER YOUR EFFING MAIL?

He received his money by return of post.

Of course, it's not often that such blatant attention-getters are called for, but the winning principle is sound.

WINNING BEFORE THE STEPS

Actors, in addition to being able to use their voices well, are less frequently caught out than most of us by that distressing phenomenon known as '*l'esprit d'escalier*' – stair-case wit – which causes its victims to think of a witty retort or crushing argument minutes after leaving a business meeting or social gathering. This is partly because actors are confident in social situations and tend to be good with words anyway, but also because, having learned a great deal of dialogue by rote, they are often able to produce a telling phrase immediately it is cued or triggered by what other people are saying.

Fortunately, winners don't need to learn vast tracts of script in order to make use of this technique because, as they usually know in advance what social or business situations will be facing them, they can often make some preparation for an important occasion.

Winners like to learn but they realise that trying to con a specialist after reading one book on his subject is not a winning move. However, they also like to be able to take an intelligent interest in the proceedings and one book *could* provide all the background that's needed. It could also give them a basis for a couple of questions, either to ask the expert or to raise in general conversation, especially if they are asked in such a way as to make the expert or fellow guest look good.

Winners often find it worthwhile to ask their host or hostess in advance about the jobs and special interests of the other guests. In any case, 'Tell me about yourself' or 'Tell me about your job' is a winning opening line in many social situations.

WINNING FOR THE RECORD

Just as we can use a tape recorder to improve the timbre of our voice or our accent, we can make use of tape to hone our conversational skills. For example, try reading a page or two of witty dialogue, either getting a friend or partner to help out or taking all the parts yourself. There are modern playscripts in most public libraries which will help improve phrasing and yield the odd usable line which can be adapted, or even quoted, provided we are prepared to give the author a nod of acknowledgement, if appropriate.

Don't forget that, if a character's witty dialogue makes you feel that you will never be a great conversationalist, the playwright may have spent all day polishing one 'spontaneous' line.

It's much the same thing with the masters of the 'ad libs', the great improvisers of dialogue, and even comedians and politicians replying to hecklers. The number of variations on any given situation is limited, and even hecklers are all too predictable, so that forethought can produce a triggered response that sounds like magic.

Teachers and other educators who cover the same ground with different students each year wait for questions they know must come and which elicit triggered responses which sound like instant wisdom, especially if preceded by a couple of seconds of what appears to be deep thought.

Winners have often worked out one or two responses to trigger words and questions in advance and find that using a tape recorder actually enables them to increase the impression of spontaneity.

Other win factors which help conversational skills are those delaying phrases which exist in all languages, like, 'Now, how shall I put this?' which provides two seconds of thinking time; or, better still, as it's a double winner, 'Well, I appreciate what you have been saying and I have to admit it is a very good argument in favour of "x" but . . .' which not only strokes your conversational partner but gives you eight seconds or so in which to come up with a response.

Sadly, some of the finest conversational delayers ever invented are now known to endanger health so, in the absence of cigarettes and pipes, winners must use ingenuity, while remembering that hurried rushes to the bathroom or clumsy handling of drinks, though effective, can only be used once.

MORE WINNING WORDS

Winning words are usually the simplest and shortest that will convey exactly the meaning we intend, but this doesn't mean that winners can get by on the vocabulary of 800 words or so which make up 'Basic English'.

Winners can improve their vocabularies by osmosis, especially if they vary their reading material, but it speeds things up if they look up in a dictionary any words that are not defined by their context, after being encountered a couple of times.

A large vocabulary helps winners to understand what they read. It also helps them to understand what they hear, but it should not be used to make other people feel like losers. Again, if you want to have a laugh at people who use words incorrectly – especially if they are pompous idiots – it's a winning move to wait until you get home.

One way of building up a winning vocabulary is to make a note of derivations when you look up words as this will often enable you to acquire a whole family of words at a time.

Incidentally everyone, but everyone, no matter how brilliant or how well educated, makes a mistake with words every now and again, especially in conversation. Winners have the confidence to laugh at their own mistakes with words – and to learn from them.

Tips from the Top

It costs nothing to be polite.

Write your 'thank you's' rather than phone. Written recognition is ten times more powerful.

He who communicates – leads.

7

WRITING TO WIN

Most winners enjoy writing – largely because, unlike most other forms of communication, it enables them to marshal their thoughts into a winning form before expressing them. They can get their brain into gear before sitting down at the typewriter or word processor and they know that, if they compose their message correctly, it will often have a greater and more permanent impact than the spoken word and that a written message is frequently the preliminary to a personal encounter and can set a winning tone for it.

Mind you – unless they are professional writers and geniuses to boot – even winners don't expect to write great prose all the time. Like journalists and advertising copy-writers, they are concerned with getting their message across. Like them, they realise that most people's attention-span is short and they follow the old Fleet Street rule: 'Get it right, keep it short, keep it crisp!'

GET IT RIGHT

Unlike the spokenword if we write something down it becomes at least semi-permanent, acquires greater legal weight and, should we get it wrong, can sometimes come back to haunt us.

Not even a genius gets it right first time every time

Winners make sure they get things right to the best of their ability, beginning with the name of the person they are writing to. They usually leave what they have written for a little while before sending it off and then check for errors of fact or language. This doesn't mean they are pedantic about grammar, especially if the 'correct' version seems stiff and unnatural, as in 'to whom they are writing', but it does mean checking names, dates, figures and spelling.

Winners pay people the compliment of getting these things right.

KEEP IT SHORT!

Brevity doesn't imply rudeness. On the contrary, a short letter often requires more thought than a long one and is therefore a compliment to the recipient. As French philosopher Blaise Pascal put it, at the end of a long and rambling letter to a friend, 'I'm sorry to have troubled you with this long letter but I'm afraid I didn't have time to write a short one.'

A winning rule of thumb for notes and business letters is to try where possible to get all that you wish to say on to one page.

If you need to introduce more than one important subject it is often worth writing several letters, which not only enables you to follow the 'keep it short', one-page rule, but also makes each of your subjects seem more important and therefore more likely to produce a winning response. Keeping letters short also helps us to concentrate our minds on the message and to avoid, for example, needless repetition. Remember that the person whose attention you are trying to capture may well be extremely busy so it is no use burying your most important point in the middle of a load of verbiage.

Winners frequently use a three-part formula of (a) gaining attention, (b) explaining the situation, (c) suggesting action. Without implying for one moment that winners should ever be terse or rude, a note reading: 'You rat, you owe me £20 – pay up immediately!' would almost certainly produce better results than a ten-page letter. Masters of the written word can be brief without a hint of rudeness: on one occasion, for example, when George Bernard Shaw was asked to quit his house, he replied, 'Dear Sir, I remain, Yours faithfully, GBS.'

KEEP IT CRISP

Winning letters are only slightly more formal in style than the equivalent spoken communication.

For some reason the Jobsworth clan, whatever heights they may attain, tend to ignore this rule, which leads to a whole Jobsworth sub-literature, ranging from hilarious reports to competely incomprehensible books of scholarship.

The trouble is that almost all of us are a little in awe of the written word, which means that we sometimes assume that a written communication must be in some way different and 'superior' to its spoken equivalent. This leads to written statements like, 'I was proceeding along Corn Street in a northerly direction when I observed two individuals of the male persuasion whose physiognomy was unknown to me,' instead of, 'I was walking north along Corn Street when I spotted two men I didn't know.'

Further up the professional ladder, bureaucratic Jobsworths are convinced that they would be placing their jobs in jeopardy – whoops! don't we mean in danger? – by producing documents which the man in the street could readily understand.

The fine American historian, Barbara Tuchman, whose own books are models of clarity, once wrote, 'Short words are always preferable to long ones, the fewer syllables the better . . . if a historian's words are not understood it is the fault of the writer.'

WINNING IN THE COMFORT ZONES

Winning words can transform a piece of paper into an ambassador to another person's comfort zone, whether it is their home or their office, which could be one of the reasons why many people find junk mail an abuse of privilege.

Of course, newly appointed ambassadors have to present their credentials and conduct themselves rather differently from those who have been in the same embassy for years. In the same way introductory letters and letters to people you don't know well have quite a different ring to those addressed to friends and long-time acquaintances.

Winners know that in most circumstances good manners and consideration for others are key factors in written communication, although there may be the rare occasion when winners feel obliged to use the written word to blast open a comfort zone and shock its inhabitants into action.

One almost guaranteed comfort-zone blaster was the telegram which was always regarded as being 'urgent'. Sadly, the ubiquitous fax machine doesn't have quite the same effect, but in some cases it could be more impressive than an ordinary letter.

A WINNING CARD

A winning move with visiting or business cards is to buy the best you can afford. Keep them uncluttered and find out the local ground rules for their use. The Japanese, for example, have a whole business-card etiquette which requires, among other things, that in order to win you must refrain from writing on the back of your card, which must also be handed over in such a way that the recipient can read it as it is being tendered.

WINNING WITH CVs

'Curriculum vitae' means 'the run of one's life' and the Germans use the word *Lebenslauf*, or 'life's run', which makes writing one sound a less daunting task.

Of course, if we were to tell the whole story we would need several books to do our 'life's course' justice, instead of a page or so – here again a single page is best – which means we need to be selective. This makes it hard work preparing a CV – as Blaise Pascal would have appreciated – but it also means that without deviating from the truth we can present ourselves in the best possible light, depending on the position we are seeking.

If you have access to a word processor, making a skeleton CV is simple – as is making any necessary additions and deletions. If not, type out a skeleton of things that will seldom be changed, leaving plenty of space between each item to make it easy to work on additions and alterations. Remember that even 'immutable' entries like your name may sometimes be changed for the better. For example if your name is William Smythe-Darcy Montmorency Davis and you are applying for a job in, say, the sanitation department of a Labour-controlled Welsh council you might fare better to call yourself plain Bill Davis on your CV.

Very often you will not need to alter your basic CV too much, except to emphasise those aspects of your life which you think may be of particular interest to a prospective employer. The essential thing is to have one handy and not wait until you have perhaps lost your job or want to change it and are not feeling too much of a winner.

Most written communications reflect the mood of the writer, so it is better to write out job applications and so on when we are feeling at our best, even if this means writing out a blanket application to go with our skeleton CV and fleshing out the details when appropriate.

MAIL IN HASTE – REPENT AT LEISURE

It is rarely a winning move to send off letters in the first flush of anger, or even enthusiasm, as both can prove costly. Far better to write them when feelings are running high – which can produce some splendidly spontaneous phrasing – and then wait a little while before reading them through, altering them if necessary and putting them in the post. Another winning idea if you have a partner is to get them to read through any letters written in anger, to give you a second opinion.

WIN WITH WHY

Ask yourself why you are writing the letter in question. The answer is unlikely to be that you are writing it to make you feel better so, once you have established the real reason for your letter, try to visualise the recipient and imagine the effect your letter will have in its original form. For example, a letter written in anger might read: 'Cutting my expenses was a lousy trick and you can stuff your rotten job.' Unless you are keen to leave and are looking for an excuse to do so this is not a winning letter, besides which winners tend to leave doors open – just in case.

Your next version might read: 'I feel deeply hurt that you should have cut my expenses and because of this will have to give serious consideration to my position with Archibald and Plinge.'

A third version could be: 'I was upset to see that my expenses had been cut and I'm writing to the hotel to ask for receipts for the items concerned. Whether I can get hold of these or not, the fact remains that I spent the money on the firm's business and would like it back.'

With the third version you stand a fair chance of getting your money – and keeping your job – which makes this the winning letter because that's what you really wanted in the first place.

WIN WITH WHO

Visualising the recipient is a good way to win with any letters – not merely angry ones. Of course it helps if you know the person concerned and, if you don't, a little reconnaissance is in order.

How much trouble you take depends to some extent on how important the letter is, but basic winning courtesy requires that you should phone if need be to find out the recipient's name, their job title and – if it is a woman – whether she likes to be addressed as Miss, Mrs or Ms.

If you know someone in the same firm, finding out what you want to know about the person you are writing to is easy. If not, a chat with their secretary on the lines of, 'I just wanted to find out whether so and so is the right person to ask about this before I contact them . . .' could produce the information you want.

WIN WITH THE MAGIC WORDS

It's easy to forget that the words that work like magic in conversation can have the same effect or greater when written down and that, for example, a note saying 'please' or 'thank you' can help make us winners. The same applies to a phrase like 'I wonder if you could help me', with the bonus that it can help overcome 'writers' block'.

Whether you are writing a short note or a full-length novel, if you find yourself staring at a pile of blank paper – or an empty screen – the way to win is to begin writing. Your first sentence may need to be changed later, it may even be complete rubbish and have to be deleted, but at least you will have made a start and once the words begin flowing they tend to go on doing so.

'I wonder if you could help me' or 'Perhaps you would be kind enough to give your advice about . . .' is not only a useful appeal to the near universal desire to have something in one's gift, but helps get the words flowing. After that it is a question of finding the winning words which will help convince the recipient that what you are asking is to their advantage.

WINNING WITH A DEFINITE 'MAYBE'

Words like 'may', 'perhaps', 'some' or 'many' can mean that the writer – or speaker – is avoiding the issue, but on occasions they can also be winners. As all journalists know, to claim that something is 'the biggest' is to invite a flood of letters pointing out that something else is even bigger – which is why they prefer to use 'among the biggest' or 'one of the biggest'.

In business communications, writing 'most of the parts were faulty' instead of 'all the parts were faulty' means that, instead of trying to find evidence of one perfect part, the onus is on the recipient either to claim that no parts were imperfect or to admit that some were imperfect and to explain why this happened. Another way to see how qualifiers can be winners is to imagine a note following a lovers' tiff in which 'you always behave unreasonably' provokes an angry reply, whereas, 'you do sometimes behave unreasonably' may allow scope for discussion – and reconciliation.

In the same way, qualifying words and expressions like 'should' or even 'will almost certainly' – as in 'should meet the deadline' – can save a lot of red faces, while still expressing confidence. *Losers promise – winners deliver*.

ACCENTUATE THE POSITIVE

By contrast, when giving instructions, the winning way is usually – spot the weasel! – to put them into a positive form. Once again it is a question of making the other person feel a winner and in this case 'do' is better than 'don't'.

Orders and instructions cast in a positive form are easier to accept so that, especially as politeness seems natural with the positive form, 'Please keep to the pathways' sounds better than 'Don't walk on the grass!'

Tips from the Top

Write your 'thank you's' quickly – before they become letters of apology.

Always try to explain why a task should be done – the other person may have a better way of performing it or producing a better result.

Know your strengths and exercise them. Don't worry about your shortcomings.

8

WINNING AT
INTERVIEWS

A winning interview is one in which all those taking part end up as winners – even if all they have gained is experience.

In job interviews, for example, there should be winners on both sides of the table but, since we are following the development of our winner as he goes out into the world, we'll begin by looking at the job interview from the point of view of the applicant.

WINNING IN ADVANCE

There's an old army saying to the effect that 'time spent in reconnaissance is seldom wasted' and this certainly applies to job applications.

Winners of course will have prepared their CVs and specimen job applications in advance; they may also have sussed out a few job opportunities long before deciding – or perhaps needing – to make a change, but it is still essential to make sure they have all the information they need and that it is still accurate.

If you haven't prepared a 'parachute', reconnaissance is doubly important and first of all winners should decide whether the job they are thinking of applying for is really the job they want.

DO YOU WANT THE JOB?

Finding out about the company will help you to decide whether you really want the job or not and while it is fine to go for an interview if you are merely unsure, it's not a winning move to carry on with your application if there are factors you know for certain would make the job unacceptable.

A vegeterian, for instance, having spotted a tempting recruiting advertisement for a manufacturing company, might well not wish to go any further with the application if he learned that the firm in question made sausages.

Another important factor is the location of the firm. After all, if it is going to take an hour to travel to work, that adds up to more than a working day a week or *two months a year*, so unless the travelling time provides, say, a convenient opportunity for study, it could mean that you wouldn't want the job if it were offered.

WINNING APPLICATIONS

Once winners have decided that they would be interested in the job, they polish up their CVs and send off an appropriate letter of application, emphasising their suitability and relevant experience.

PREPARING A WINNING CV

If you are past school-leaving age and have lots of relevant experience or higher educational qualifications, don't lean too heavily on details of your GCSE or A-level attainments. Do stress any communication or mathematical skills, together with any extra-curricular activities that indicate initiative, energy or leadership skills.

One winning plan is to put yourself in the interviewer's shoes and imagine him reading your CV. You may then realise that having won the finger-painting prize at St Mungo's Infants may not help him to evaluate your potential as a computer salesman.

If you are sent a printed application form it is permissible to accentuate the things that make you a potential candidate while skating over those which might make you unsuitable. However, *only losers lie*, which doesn't mean that all winners are saints but merely that it is often all too easy to trip up – which makes truth the winning option.

Try to get your CV on one page if possible and make sure that the points you want to emphasise come over clearly. If you are applying to an American firm it's worth noting that many American CVs place the most recent information – such as qualifications and experience – *first* instead of in chronological order. Draw up a specimen CV and use this as your master copy to be adapted and added to, according to the job you are applying for.

SPECIMEN CV

CURRICULUM VITAE

Name: MICHAEL ANYBODY
Date and place of birth: 15 December 1962, Anytown, Yorkshire
Address: 27 Plinge Road, Anytown

EDUCATION
Dates . . . Secondary School 'O' & 'A' levels (if obtained)
Dates . . . Further Education: Colleges, Universities, Polytechnics,
etc. Any qualification obtained.

JOBS
Anything relevant during vacations or full time up to present.
Date . . . Job . . . description if relevant
Date . . . Job
Date . . . Job . . . (Also took evening course in . . .)

INTERESTS
Travel . . . details . . . Sport . . . details . . . Active   member   of
(theatre group, charity organisation, etc. etc.).

Always take a clean copy of your CV with you. It allows you to be helpful if interviewers have mislaid their copy and will be of tremendous help if you are asked to fill in a questionnaire as you will have all the basic information like dates to hand and be able to spend more time on the other questions.

Many firms place a great deal of weight on these profiles, even though some of them seem designed to eliminate winners. We know one chap, for example, whose application to join the staff of a major insurance company was turned down because he was 'too shy'. Asked to answer 'YES' or 'NO' to the question, 'Would you push to the front of a bus queue in which people were jostling for position?' he had answered honestly, 'NO'. There was no space for him to add that as a 6'1" tall, rugger-playing ex-Commando he rarely found it necessary to behave other than court-eously, so he was judged to lack assertiveness.

The moral is that if you want the job you don't have to tell your potential employers what you think they want to hear – but you should bear it in mind.

BE PREPARED

Once winners have decided they want the job they will take the time to prepare. It's worthwhile, for example, trying to talk to someone who has been to an interview with the same firm. It's on the cards that they will still be using much the same methods and that in a smallish firm one or per-haps all of the interviewers may be the same people.

Next, try a couple of dummy interviews using a tape recorder and, if possible, get a friend or partner to play the part of the interviewer. Work out – using the knowledge of the firm you have been able to gain – some of the questions they are almost bound to ask.

These might include: 'What do you know about us?' 'Why do you want to work for us?' 'What were the subjects you liked or disliked at school?' 'You mention amateur dramatics – Do you act? Do you direct?' 'Are you inter-ested in sports?' 'Do you enjoy working in a team?'

If you are able to work with a partner get them to ask the questions you have discussed and then to bowl you a 'googly', a tricky unexpected question, and see how you make out.

If you have heard that the firm use the 'good cop – nasty cop' technique, with one sympathetic interviewer and one complete bastard, you should practise answering questions put in an unsympathetic way. 'Just why did you leave your last position?' or 'Exactly why do you want to leave your present job? Are you having difficulty handling the work?' could be examples.

Remember that the interviewers will usually be playing on their home ground and that they may well have conducted hundreds of similar interviews, so it's a winning move to put in some practice. The tape recorder will give you an indication of how much you have improved.

THINK WINNING

Because they have prepared themselves in advance, winners are unlikely to panic when faced with the real interview, but there are one or two things worth considering.

Winners, for example, think ahead. They have already imagined themselves doing the job for which they are being interviewed and this – without their being conscious of it – gives their approach confidence. It even changes their choice of words so that instead of, 'If I get the job, would I be required to . . .?' they might say, 'Would my responsibilities include . . .?'

Another reason winners do not panic is that they have convinced themselves of an important truth, namely that if – by some incredible stroke of misfortune – they do not get the job, they are unlikely to be taken out and shot. *To a winner, a disappointment is not the same thing as a tragedy.*

Some winners do suffer from nerves. After all, many winning actors still get stage fright even after years in the theatre and claim it helps their performance. Interviews, whichever side of the table you are on, are a performance, but if you do feel nervous, provided you are certain that you won't dissolve into helpless mirth, try to imagine the interviewers naked.

BOTH SIDES WANT TO WIN

The most important thing to remember is that unless the job has already gone to the chairman's niece or nephew, the interviewers want to win for themselves and their company. This makes it highly unlikely that they have decided to waste an hour or so of their time at immense cost to their company in making the applicants look idiots.

It's much more likely that they wish to finish the day with a warm winning glow and the chance to report to their superiors that, after interviewing some excellent candidates, they have come up with someone who seems ideal for the job.

WINNING ON THE DAY

Winners are relaxed. As holistic winners they are aware of their own value, their membership of a winning team at home and the fact that they have a comfort zone to return to – whatever happens.

They have prepared themselves by role-playing and are psychologically prepared for a meeting rather than a contest.

As winners, they have selected – and tried on – the outfit they are wearing, which is of course appropriate and comfortable, and they are clean, neat and looking good.

One distinctive – but not garish – item of clothing or jewellery is permissible. It will enable the interviewers to identify you immediately when it comes to the post-interview inquest.

WINNERS TRAVEL FIRST

Winners travel to interviews first class and they would rather spend money on a taxi than arrive looking wet and bedraggled. If you can't manage first-class fares and taxis, arrange to look as if you have travelled in style by arriving early and using the firm's cloakroom. If it is at all feasible you should have timed your journey to the interview, door to door, a few days in advance and have positively identified your destination. There are few things worse than arriving on the dot, only to be told, 'Ah, yes, this is So-and-So Hall but you want So-and-So House. It's about three miles down the road.' If a physical reconnaissance is out of the question, make some careful telephone inquiries.

WINNING WHILE WAITING

Winners don't mind waiting a little while – too long and they expect an explanation and an apology, not to mention a cup of coffee – because they can use the time to read the company's latest brochures and to ask the receptionist about the names and composition of the interviewing panel, together with their job titles. If the commissionaires and receptionists are obviously members of the Jobsworth family this may tell you something about the company but, whatever they seem like at the moment, you should already be thinking of them as potential friends and allies for the day you walk in through the door as a fellow employee.

WINNING FACE TO FACE

Because they look good, feel good and are well prepared, winners walk into interviews with confidence. Their posture is good and their speech clear and direct. *Winners remember that they are applicants not supplicants*.

Body language should reflect relaxed alertness, not tension – no folded arms, for instance. You have something to sell to people you know are in the market and as a winner you are certain you have a great product.

The interviewers' attitude can tell you quite a lot about the company. You are entitled to expect politeness from the panel, a preliminary effort to put you at ease and, eventually, a chance to put questions to the interviewers. Winners stress what they will be able to do for the company but they also want to know what the company will do for them. This doesn't mean, however, that your very first question should be about the company car.

Winners leave interviewers with the impression that they have found the right person for the job – someone who is prepared to make a real contribution, who puts job satisfaction and scope for eventual advancement high on the priority list and who will fit into the team.

WINNERS FOLLOW THROUGH

Winners try for a natural exit-line which should always include a 'thank you' and which, like a Guards tie or a

Hermes scarf, helps them to follow through to the 'inquest' on candidates – which may not even take place on the same day. Winners don't leave interviewers wondering, 'Now then, so-and-so – which one was that?'

One way of following through, if you didn't get the job but still feel you would have liked it, is to write to the senior interviewer, thanking the interviewer once again, saying how disappointed you were and asking if they would be kind enough to help you by letting you know where you went wrong, especially as you were trained at . . . etc. etc. This letter could elicit useful information, but the winning factor is that it gives you a second chance to summarise your case and to let them know that if their chosen candidate breaks a leg, or if there is a similar opening in the future, you are still interested.

WINNING ON THE INTERVIEWER'S SIDE OF THE TABLE

Interviews, in addition to providing a splendid chance to recruit exciting new winners for your team, are also a PR exercise. Presumably you have already weeded out the deadlegs by mail so every candidate, even if not selected, is a potential ambassador for your organisation. 'I was sorry not to get the job with Plinge International – the people who interviewed me made it sound a terrific outfit to work for' is a winning result. 'I wouldn't work for those bastards for twice what they're offering and a Rolls as a company car' is not.

Interviewers have obvious power. Winning interviewers do not make their power obvious.

Making candidates sweat is not a winning move. An

ordinary interview should be enough to test their reaction to stress. If you feel you have to subject them to the third degree to find out if they could stand the stress of working for your company, your next winning move would be to take a long hard look at your company and how it goes about its business.

Using interviews to 'blood' interviewers when the position has already been filled is terrible PR.

Winning interviewers and winning organisations give every candidate – and themselves – a chance to win.

Tips from the Top

The three ingredients of success are: stamina, stamina and stamina.

If you can keep someone working for you who is cleverer than you, then actually you are cleverer than them.

Winning is the natural outcome of a positive attitude.

9

WAYS TO WIN AT WORK

Most of us spend half our waking lives working or preparing for work and in many cases work dominates the rest of our time by determining where and how we shall live, what sort of people we meet and what sort of lives our children are going to have. This means that if we are to be holistic winners, winning in all departments of our lives, we have to win at work.

It also suggests that some of us could be in danger of allowing our work to become too important so that, instead of merely influencing our lives, it dominates them, controls them – and in some cases, ruins them.

WINNERS WORK AS LITTLE AS POSSIBLE

We suggested in *How to be a Winner* that one way to be a winner at work was to stop working but this was by no means an idlers' charter.

Work, we argued, was the expenditure of physical and mental energy on things that we usually didn't want to do, as opposed to 'employment' – much of which could and should be enjoyable. We should also have pointed out that people who enjoy what they are doing invariably perform better than those who find their jobs 'hard work', and that the sort of bosses who insist, 'You're not here to enjoy yourselves,' are fated to be losers. Jobsworth & Co. may feel that their employees' time is bought and paid for but if times get hard it's the workers who have been enjoying their jobs who will want to save them by helping their company to remain a winner.

EVEN WINNERS WORK – SOMETIMES

Most people have to do some work, whether they are employed, self-employed or even unemployed. There is almost always some task or activity which has to be tackled when we would really rather be doing something else.

Fortunately, one person's work is another's fun and vice versa, so that travelling round the world might be sheer hell to one person and a constant delight for someone else. At the same time there are people who get a kick out of writing reports or balancing books.

This means that, if we are to be winners, it is immensely important to choose the right job, namely one in which the things we like doing – and which therefore cannot be considered 'work' – outweigh those things we don't particularly enjoy.

WINNERS KNOW WHEN TO LEAVE

If everything about a particular job is hard work in the sense that we don't enjoy it at all, then the only winning move is to move, either within the organisation or out of it altogether because, contrary to the popular saying, hard work can kill you.

Mind you, it is unlikely to kill you in a week or a month so there is time – if you have not already done so – to prepare a 'parachute', by fixing yourself up with a job you are sure you will enjoy before you quit the job you don't.

Even winners have the occasional Black Monday but if you wake up hating the thought of going to work every single day – leave.

WINNERS MAKE FRIENDS

It's surprising how often even normally friendly folk seem to go out of their way to annoy people at work, especially those they consider to be lower in the scheme of things than themselves. Winners, on the other hand, without being either ingratiating or condescending, make friends at all levels through the firm. Merely by being reasonably pleasant they are often able to get even the most crabby of Jobsworths on their side which, considering that the Jobsworth creed involves hating everyone, is quite a feat.

In fact, winners often find it surprisingly easy to get on with Jobsworths and to enlist them as willing members of their official – or unofficial – team, simply because they take them off guard by treating them as human beings.

MAKING THE WORKPLACE A COMFORT ZONE

As we've seen, winners make their homes into comfort zones and if they travel to work by car they ensure that the vehicle is a movable comfort zone. The next step to becoming a holistic winner is to make certain that the workplace is a comfort zone.

Often physical comfort and well-being is the easiest to achieve and, in the spirit of holistic winning, will boost efforts to make the workplace a comfort zone in other respects. Individual winners build up their physical comfort zones in different ways but one obvious method is to personalise one's space.

Obviously, if you have your own office and complete control over its furnishings and decor, your workplace can become a winning tool as well as a comfort zone. It should reflect the winning personality you wish to project without being intimidating. Power decorating went out with Hitler – or should have done – so forget the long walk to your desk, the bright light shining in the face of your visitors, the uncomfortable chair or even the 'sink out of sight' armchair. Winners, who are all you want on your team, are up to such dodges anyway and can change most of them to suit themselves with a polite, 'Excuse me.'

If you have an office but not total control, you can personalise your environment and make it into a comfort zone by introducing a personal element, especially something from your home comfort zone like a favourite picture, flower vase, plant, china cup and saucer, or even a hat rack.

A COMFORT-ZONE DESK

Many people nowadays work in open-plan offices where a desk is the only private space and anyone who wants to see how comfort zones evolve almost automatically should take a look at a new open-plan office after a couple of weeks of occupation and see how the screens, notice boards, filing cabinets, pot plants and the like have appeared as if from nowhere to mark off personal or group comfort zones.

Most winners need only one item to personalise a desk comfort zone. We know one man for example who has an expensive-looking gold, ballpoint pen, in an equally impressive stand, which he says makes him feel and act like a winner every time he picks it up.

Whether they have a palatial office or a battered metal-topped desk, winners who spend any amount of time sitting down should insist on a decent, well designed chair. A badly designed chair can not only make you feel like a loser but will almost certainly make you ill, and an employer who can't appreciate that sorting out this problem is an example of winning in which both sides gain and nobody loses should be regarded as a potential ex-employer.

WINNERS RESPECT THE COMFORT ZONE

The comfort zone is an important part of winning in the workplace – so much so that winners instinctively respect other people's comfort zones whether they are private offices or desks.

The man from upstairs or the Head Office big-wig may feel like a winner when he pre-empts a subordinate's chair and puts his feet on the desk. He doesn't know that his actions may well be considered tantamount to rape and pillage and could result in seething resentment, lasting as long as both parties are with the company.

Even executives who are aware of office etiquette and who treat other people's offices much as they would their homes sometimes behave badly when they invade small comfort zones like desks.

Winners realise that in many cases the smaller and less impressive the comfort zone the more fiercely it is cherished. They realise that a simple 'May I?' or 'Do you mind?' – even on some occasions a mere gesture – before perching on the edge of someone's desk or using their phone makes both parties winners.

Strangely enough, it doesn't matter a damn if the space invaders concerned actually own the desk, the phone or even the building. The inhabitant of the comfort zone will almost always be upset if it is invaded, which means that even people who own businesses have to be careful.

BUILD A COMFORT-ZONE TEAM

Workplaces build up teams – which become comfort zones – almost automatically and winners encourage this camaraderie, while being keenly aware that it also induces a 'them and us' spirit which may have its downside. A winning organisation is built up of interacting teams which may well be competitive but should never be mutually destructive. If you want to see a real winner at work, watch the person who is welcomed with a smile and a cup of coffee by other teams as they set about helping solve his or her problem, and compare it with the way teams close ranks as soon as a member of the Jobsworth clan comes into view.

WIN WITHOUT TRYING

The great thing about winning is the way that wins grow like snowballs and winners appear to be winning without trying. For example, the winner's ability to build a team and move around other interacting teams will often bring promotion as a bonus. Another bonus is the holistic winners' attitude which suggests that they know they have potential and are quietly confident that it will be recognised. However, there are a few people who mistake happiness for lack of ambition so it can pay to let your immediate superior know – preferably in a social context – that, while you love what you are doing, you are open to offers.

WINNERS ARE YES-MEN

Like the bank in the ad, winners love to say 'yes', and 'yes, I'll certainly try, but it's going to be tough' sounds much better than 'can't be done'.

Winners behave as if they own the firm in so far as they are keen – if only for their own comfort – to have everything run efficiently and smoothly, and are prepared to input suggestions to save time, money and even paper clips.

Winning bosses recognise this and stimulate it, so if your boss isn't interested or shows no enthusiasm for ideas you could be in the wrong job.

Of course, it helps if there's a participation scheme but winning bosses know there is no such thing as a small idea and treat people at all levels as if they are part-owners of the firm. Winners are always prepared to listen.

WINNERS LIKE LOOT

Most winners like cash as much as the next person which is just as well as it often seems to flow in their direction. They are even prepared to commit 'work' by selling some of their valuable time doing things they don't find particularly pleasant or amusing, in order to fund a decent standard of living for themselves or their families. However, they are not prepared to make themselves ill or unhappy just for cash, which means that for winners there is a limit to the cash incentive.

Some organisations still use cash to implement a carrot-and-stick policy, paying big money and persuading their staff to spend every penny of it, while holding the threat of dismissal over their heads, so that every Friday night becomes a 'night of the long envelopes'. Winners tend to leave such companies fairly quickly, especially as there is often a sick, sadistic atmosphere about them. On the other hand, high-flying young winners with few commitments can enjoy big money, high-risk jobs where the stress and uncertainty are all part of the game. For them, like newsmen in Fleet Street when it *was* Fleet Street, the excitement is more important than the money.

Most winning firms have to find different ways of making the workplace exciting or at least less boring than it might be and a huge industry has grown up to help them do just this. Motivation experts know for example that being part of an improvement scheme makes people winners.

MOTIVATING WINNERS

Nick Thornely's company, Industrial Motivation, designs campaigns to encourage people to take a greater interest in their work and become more committed to the success of their organisation in such a way that both they and the organisation end up as winners.

Their particular style of motivation is to ask all employees to submit ideas on how to improve their performance and they make it clear that they are not looking for 100 per cent improvement. In fact the improvement could be as small as one per cent but the important thing is that everyone from the MD to the newest recruit to the office or shop floor should take part.

To create the right climate for the campaign they use teamwork, competition and recognition and because they believe work should be as much fun as possible they use humour to arouse interest, to break down the barriers between departments and to eliminate any feelings of 'them' and 'us'.

With their QED campaign, for example, people are asked to dream up their own interpretation of the acronym before they are told what the campaign is about. 'Quit Executive Drinking' and 'Question Every Decision' are a couple of the more polite versions.

Industrial Motivation also introduces a team structure with teams of no more than ten members to combat the feeling of being 'just a number' common in large organisations and they encourage friendly rivalry in the generation and implementation of ideas.

They find that people derive enormous satisfaction from dreaming up even small improvements and that their satisfaction is still greater when they see their ideas put into practice. Enlisting everyone's help in this way is relatively new in the UK but the Japanese have a well-established system they call *Kaizen* meaning 'continual improvement involving everyone'.

Industrial Motivation use the sort of winning concepts

we discuss in this book to create the right climate for their campaigns, to enlist the help of the self-motivated minority, to overcome the inertia of the 80 per cent who are ready to be motivated and to win over the small band of cynics and Jobsworths who are ready to sneer at any initiatives.

They overcome any worries on the part of the staff that ideas may be seen as critical of management by enlisting everyone in the campaign and avoid any fear of rejection by making sure that everyone knows their ideas will be welcome – whether they are implemented or not. They also thank everyone for their ideas and don't attempt to put a financial value on ideas that amount essentially to self-improvement.

Another application of the 'winners' principles is to build deadlines into the campaigns in order to overcome apathy.

Again, in order to point out the importance of making other people and other departments 'winners', campaigns stress that ultimately it is the customer who pays everybody's wages. However, because external customers sometimes seem remote and therefore 'someone else's problem', people should identify their main 'internal' customers, imagine that it is they who are paying the wages and focus their attention on improving their service to them.

The aim is to help people to win as individuals and as members of a team, thus creating a winning organisation, which in turn provides the climate and opportunity for individual wins. Holistic organisational winning, in fact.

WINNING WITH IDEAS

Winners know that 'taking time to become rich' means they should spare a few minutes each day to allow ideas and even completely 'off the wall' thoughts to float into their consciousness.

However, while there is no such thing as too many ideas, some winners do find themselves too interested in new ideas to follow any through. The only answer is to pick a winning idea – and go for it.

Tips from the Top

Always work to a deadline. If you have forever to do something, it will take – forever!

When you hire the hands use the brains that come with them.

Quality. Quality is making goods that don't come back for customers who do.

Employ the eccentric. Those who are only comfortable with subordinates who agree with them will not survive.

10

WINNING WHEN THE SKY FALLS IN

Winners sometimes appear to inhabit a different world from other people – a world in which there are fewer bastards, fewer shambles and fewer instances of rank bad luck.

In fact, winners live in the same world as the rest of us, an imperfect world full of villainous men in black hats, obstructive Jobsworths and sportive fates whose idea of humour is to let someone win the ship's lottery on the *Titanic*.

It's merely that winners are usually better able to cope with the world because they are able both to modify it slightly and to prepare for its vicissitudes.

BEATING THE BASTARDS

There's an old saying which goes '*nihil illigitimae carborundum*' or 'don't let the bastards grind you down!' which is excellent winning advice always provided you have correctly identified the illegitimates in question.

Unfortunately, bastards come in all shapes and sizes ranging from Jobsworths – whose family tree often has a hint of the bar sinister – to the thorough-going copper-bottomed bastards with a short 'a' in the first syllable.

As we've seen, winners frequently succeed in recruiting run-of-the-mill Jobsworths to their official or unofficial teams but Jobsworths who have a yellow belt in bastardy can be trickier to deal with.

Linguistic judo on the lines of 'You're absolutely right about that, but . . .' can often be helpful with these low-grade illegitimates, and even those in positions of some authority, as can the implication that the winner is a member or the leader of a winning team as in, 'We think we ought to . . .'.

Often a winner's attitude – derived from a winning sense of inner worth, a winning partnership and a winning home base – is enough to defeat these minor villains.

WINNERS WON'T FIGHT

Winners won't fight – unless it's absolutely necessary. Like the man in the white hat in the classic Western movies, winners would rather talk than rush into a confrontation.

Winners, for example, will always explore the possibility that there has been a misunderstanding. There's always the chance that the other person is behaving like a bastard because he thinks – wrongly – that he has been cheated, badly done by, made to look small or otherwise affronted. A great many battles in the workplace – and even in social situations – can be avoided by winners saying something like, 'I'm sorry we seem to have got off on the wrong foot. Let's get together over a drink and see if we can't make a fresh start.'

Other battles which may not need to be fought are those against seeming bastards who are ordinary people who are simply having a bad day – or for that matter a bad year. Here again, winners who are willing to spend time on reconnaissance could discover, for example, that the 'bastard' in question has been facing illness, personal tragedy or an emotional crisis at home and is taking it out on everybody he meets. Of course, it could merely be that his pet budgie has died but if that is a tragedy to him it could easily affect his behaviour.

People are not always what they seem and we know of one boss whose red nose and fierce demeanour caused him to be regarded as a bad-tempered drunk, if not a complete bastard, by those who did not know that he was a teetotal lay preacher who was suffering from a painful illness.

To understand everything may not quite be to forgive everything, as the saying suggests, but it does help winners to adopt a winning stance.

WINNERS CAN FIGHT

The French have a splendid expression for wimps and pushovers; they call them *poires* or pears – meaning the fat mushy variety you can poke your finger through.

Winners, of course, are not *poires*; they prefer not to fight but they can fight better than most if they have to and, while they may feel obliged to allow their adversary the first strike, they will rarely turn the other cheek. Like the man in the white hat, winners try hard to find another way before buckling on their guns but, like the good guy in the movies, when they do so they invariably have the advantage of surprise. Winners don't even raise their voices most of the time so that, when they do, people tend to listen, while if winners talk harshly the bad guys are often struck dumb with surprise and behave as if their pet gerbil had taken a bite out of their leg.

Of course, winners have more than surprise going for them. Once they've checked that the bad guy's illegitimacy is the real thing and have run out of excuses for his behaviour, they will plan a verbal or tactical counter-attack which will hit him hard. Incidentally, as winners, they will have built up a well-deserved reputation for decency so their rare sneaky move will be regarded by observers as a legitimate *ruse de guerre*. They will also have tried to recruit the townsfolk – or in this case their fellow employees – so that, come High Noon, they don't have to stand alone.

SEX IN THE WORKPLACE

Anyone who wishes to take sex out of the workplace wants to take the fun out of life and winners certainly don't want that. Winners know they can use sex appeal to win even quite important victories with a smile. They also tend to enjoy the sort of banter which goes on in some offices with everyone giving as good – or bad – as they get. Many a time these exchanges, especially if they are based on 'in' references, reinforce the notion of a winning team.

Again, few winners would seek to ban dating among people who work in the same organisation, although apart from the lightning strike of a *coup de foudre* which few people can resist or the attraction that grows over a long period of time spent working together, it would seem sensible to limit socialising with immediate colleagues to group occasions.

WINNERS HATE HARASSMENT

What is totally abhorrent to any winner is sexual blackmail or harassment in any guise and whichever sex is doing the harassing. Winners can usually prevent this sort of thing from starting by promoting the right atmosphere and by recruiting in advance allies who will be useful in this sort of emergency.

Winners try to nip in the bud any tendency among potential harassers to 'see how far they can go' because if they are allowed to continue things can only get worse.

Acting early can prevent the sort of persistent nastiness which makes life uncomfortable – even unbearable – and which can be more difficult to counter than physical harassment for which there is now legal redress.

Unfortunately, real life is not a Western movie and there are occasions when the bad guys are too numerous, or too powerful, to beat, in which case the only winning move is to leave town – although, of course, winners being human, it is often possible to 'dynamite' the place before riding out.

Mind you, to keep the analogy to the bitter end, in a decent town it's the sheriff and the mayor who should be wearing white hats, and in a winning company it is up to the managers at every level to make sure that sexism, racism, ageism and the rest do not get started.

PARACHUTES AND SUCH

Winners are confident and optimistic almost by definition but they do cast an occasional glance at the sky to see if it is firmly in place because not to do so is an indication of 'hubris' – the sort of pride which goes before a fall into the deep manure.

They think about – but do not worry about – what they would do if the worst were to happen and employ this Worst Possible Scenario technique even on relatively minor issues.

Winners know what they would do if someone suggested moving their office or their desk, they know what they would do if the company went bust overnight or if they were made redundant, because they have played the Worst Possible Scenario game regarding most issues which might one day become of importance to them.

This will often make winners look like super winners by preventing them from going to war over trivia because they will have decided in advance that certain issues are not matters of life and death. They will also have decided in broad outline on which issues they feel it would be necessary to make a stand.

Like the war-time pilots who knew that any landing they could walk away from was a good one, they have their priorities worked out and know that life and health are the most important things.

They will also have concluded in advance – because when the sky does fall in it is often too late – that time really does heal a great many wounds. You may not be laughing about your misfortunes in six months' time but by God you will almost always be surprised that you once considered suicide an option.

Winners' 'parachutes', in case the firm folds or they are made redundant, include preparations like being aware of other job openings, having a hobby which can be made to provide an income, knowing how little they and the family, if they have one, can live on. In some cases non-working or part-time working partners may have decided what contribution they could make by, say, going out to work full time, if only for a limited period.

A TROUBLE SHARED CAN BE A TROUBLE ENDED

Winners are prepared to talk over any troubles they may have with partners, relatives and friends. This can not only mean the trouble being shared but can avoid having people say, when it is much too late, 'If only I had known – I could have lent you a few quid, found you a new job . . .' or whatever. Almost without being aware of it, winners will have built up a network of friends and acquaintances with whom they are in credit when it comes to good turns and, although sometimes these creditors will default at the crucial moment, there is often some store of goodwill that can be called upon when needed. However, even people who owe you favours won't always be able to divine that you are in trouble unless you let them know the score.

WINNERS BOUNCE BACK

One characteristic all winners share is the ability to bounce back when their world has crumbled around them and to rebuild their lives – often better than before.

Whether they lose their money or their business, are struck down by dreadful illness or fail at the very moment of completing some cherished enterprise, winners will pick themselves up and – often within a remarkably short period of time – will be well on the way to another success.

Winners bounce back

Often their second major endeavour bears little or no relation to their original enterprise but, remarkably, their success will usually be at the same level. In material terms, for example, a millionaire winner on whom the sky falls may lose all his money but when he builds up a new business he will not usually make himself merely comfortable or even wealthy. He will be on his way to a new million – and almost certainly more.

This ability to bounce back is due in part to the holistic winner's conviction of his own worth and his wins in areas not affected by the collapse of the sky. However, the main reason is that winning is not only cumulative but habit-forming, so that winners become accustomed to winning, at whatever level they operate, and will usually go back to winning at that level even after a serious reverse.

BOUNCING WINNERS

Most of us know at least one person who has bounced back. Politician Jeffrey Archer, for example, whose life appeared to be in ruins when he was faced with more than half a million pounds' worth of debts, changed career to become a best-selling author, paid back all that he owed and went on to make millions.

Then there's heavyweight boxer Frank Bruno who in spite of putting up a courageous showing was defeated by Mike Tyson. Years later Frank, who interestingly never lost his winner's status in the eyes of the public, is still thinking about whether or not he will ever put on the gloves in earnest again. Meanwhile he has embarked on a new and successful career as an actor and TV personality and has managed to turn what was once regarded as an unfortunate speech habit into an instantly recognisable trade mark – 'Know what I mean, Harry?'

A bouncing winner in a slightly more conventional mode is former property developer Charles Ware whose enviable millionaire life-style once included an ultra des. res. in Bath's Royal Crescent. When he was wiped out by the mini-slump which ruined so many of his colleagues, Charles turned his hand to restoring Morris Minors and now has a thriving international business. Restoring the mini-classic has already restored his fortunes but, typically, he now plans to become an even bigger winner by manufacturing 100mph-plus Morris Minors with state-of-the-art technical specifications and performance.

This sort of resilience when the sky falls in is a bonus all winners share and goes hand in hand with the adaptability which enables them to avoid the comfort-zone trap.

Tips from the Top

The shortest cut is often the longest way.

Profit with fun.

When the going gets tough, the tough get going.

Don't tell me the *ten* reasons why something can't be done. Tell me the *one* reason why it can.

11

WINNING AWAY

Building up comfort zones, by increasing our self-esteem, by making our partners and our families winners and by recruiting a winning team in the workplace, is an essential part of holistic winning.

Unfortunately, ever since we were expelled from our first comfort zone after nine months or so of warm, safe, carefree existence, most of us have been a little reluctant to leave any substitute comfort zone we may have found.

This is why – although the term itself is useful – we prefer to regard the comfort zones as comfort 'bases' from which we can sally forth to conquer new and exciting worlds.

This doesn't mean that there is anything wrong with building up our bases – far from it – but only that remaining in the womb, however comfortable, is hardly a winning tactic.

Birth is the real victory, and if later we build ourselves cocoons they should not be prisons but places in which we prepare for changes which will allow us to face a more interesting and challenging life.

So far we have looked at several comfort zones and shown how they can be used as bases when we begin to spread our wings but, in fact, leaving our comfort zones is an essential part of the winning process. Fortunately it is also, as a rule, something we are able to practise.

PASSING FIRST BASE

When it comes to comfort zones some people never get past first base, which may well make them comfortable but does little to make them holistic winners.

Such people realise that no one with low self-esteem can be a winner but that is as far as they go. Believing that building up their regard for themselves is all they need to do, they puff up their self-esteem, sometimes to the point of egomania, without realising that they have exchanged one prison for another, even though a life of self-adoration may be fractionally more fun for the person concerned than one spent in feeling inferior to the rest of humanity.

People who have a life-long, exclusive love affair with themselves have only themselves to blame if other people regard them as losers rather than winners. However, it's easy enough to see how this can happen especially in the case of people who began with low self-worth but have managed to increase their self-esteem. Comfort zones are comfortable by definition and, especially if you have just created one for yourself, the temptation to stay put is enormous.

That's why, especially if we have only recently begun to improve our self-worth, we should put our still-fragile comfort zone to the test by leaving it in order to interact with our family or friends before it hardens into a restricting and impenetrable shell.

Fortunately most of us are able to practise this sort of interaction from a very early age and begin acquiring social skills long before we go to school. At home a rough and ready mix of parental indulgence and scolding usually provides a base from which to approach a perhaps similar mix of affection and competitive squabbling on the part of siblings, while they prepare us to meet our peers in the classroom and playground. Ideally these in turn provide a preparation for winning adulthood.

BIRDS DO IT

Most birds seem to equip their young for life outside the nest without any trouble but, sadly, we humans don't always find it so easy to help children become winners and sometimes it seems as if parents, families and teachers are conspiring to shatter the youngsters' self-esteem and turn them into losers.

The cold comfort zones of some childhoods range from sniping criticisms of the 'you'll never amount to anything' and 'you and your stupid ideas' type to neglect or downright abuse.

Parents should realise that all children need stroking both physically and verbally and that almost all children respond splendidly to encouragement. Teachers too should remember that praise is one of the best ways to make a child a winner but at the same time both parents and teachers should remember that most kids are hyper-sensitive to the aroma of bullshit, and look very hard for things they can praise with sincerity.

For young people who find themselves in an unbearable situation – and we don't mean having to help with the washing up – the only winning answer is to leave as soon as possible.

However, it is just as important for younger people in such a situation to have a 'parachute' as it is for grown ups. Running away to join a circus, for example, provided the circus has offered you a job, could be a winning move –

after all Cary Grant made it – but just running away is a potentially dangerous move.

If possible all young adults including – and perhaps even especially – those whose homes are genuine comfort zones should make deliberate forays from the nest – if possible with the full agreement of their parents. They could begin by spending a night with relatives who live some way away, then weekends camping with friends and graduate to spending a month or so working abroad.

LEAVING THE NEST

Most people will have tried their wings a little before becoming teenagers and certainly before reaching adulthood but only the winners will have taught themselves to soar.

Winners know that while it is a winning move to travel outwards from a home comfort zone to a workplace comfort zone, both zones should be bases rather than bomb shelters and there should certainly be no feeling that they are moving from one restricting space to another.

Unfortunately there are a great many pressures on people of all ages which combine with their own inertia to ensure that their comfort zones are on a horizontal plane.

In other words there is a tendency to gravitate towards schoolfriends on the same intellectual and social level as our immediate family, and – often influenced by the desperately low achievement levels regarded as appropriate by some schools – to take a job alongside the same sort of people with whom we have spent our early lives.

Fortunately, a great many of today's young people have realised that although there was a time – not all that long ago – when people were expected to 'know their place' and remain in it, things have changed a great deal.

However, there is still an enormous residue of class prejudice and class consciousness about and winners must learn how to deal with it, preferably from an early age.

NOT IN OUR STARS

Winners know that there is no such thing as their 'place' and they very soon become aware that many people have found that being born into a disadvantaged social class has given them the stimulus they required to make them into winners.

They know that the social level into which they were born has a class tag, long before they learn about the As and the Bs, but they also know that, if they are to become holistic winners, they must not allow themselves to be categorised and restricted – even though our class very often provides us with a ready-made comfort zone.

PRACTICE FLIGHTS

We knew one intelligent young woman who seemed so charming and poised we were astounded to discover that she felt unable to shop in one particular store because it was 'middle class'. Fortunately her talents soon gave her sufficient confidence to be able to laugh at the embarrassment she had feared as a youngster but the real surprise came when we were discussing fears of this sort with a chap we knew to be a millionaire. 'Oh yes,' he said readily,

'I still feel uncomfortable when I go into one London shop. I have the impression they are looking down on me.'

Winners know that it's only natural to feel a little apprehensive about the unknown and the unusual and go out of their way to overcome any fears they may have by deliberately moving out of their base.

However, they appreciate that in the main such shifts up – or down – the social scale are best undertaken in gradual stages. If, for example, the high spot of our social life to date has been a visit to a local fast-food restaurant we could be forgiven for feeling a little out of place in a 'posh' restaurant, while those of us accustomed to hotel cocktail bars might feel uncomfortable in a back-street pub.

Strangely, as winners soon become aware, establishments at both the upper and lower limits of the social spectrum are frequently more welcoming to cross-socialisers than those in the middle range. All you need in most spit and sawdust pubs and most of the world's finest hotels are appropriate clothes, enough money to pay for your drinks and reasonably good manners. The middle ground tends to be more difficult, no matter from which side we approach it, but even so the winning move is usually to progress up or down the scale fairly slowly so that in the end we become winners at this particular game – social chameleons who are at home anywhere.

CHAMELEONS IN THE WORKPLACE

Becoming a social chameleon is a lot of fun and once again in the spirit of holistic winning there's a bonus. There are many jobs and professions where the ability to talk to people in all walks of life is an essential qualification and, even if your contacts in the workplace are limited, it pays to be at ease when talking either to the office boy or the managing director.

Obviously the ability to socialise at all levels can pay winning dividends in the workplace and these are far from being limited to sharing a lift with the chairman.

Social skills of this sort enable us to leave our base in the workplace and sally forth into other people's comfort zones and, here again, it is often a good idea to take this type of foray in easy stages – perhaps by, wherever possible, visiting or socialising with people in departments that are similar to our own. However, after a while, winners should be at ease in every section of their organisation, even those which are staffed mainly by people of the opposite sex or from different backgrounds – perhaps even both.

This sort of winning, as much as any other, becomes a habit, so much so that, often in a remarkably short time, winners have built up a network of friends and acquaintances throughout the organisation in which they happen to be working. This can in itself lead to a promotion and often makes life much easier once promotion has been achieved and the winner has responsibility for several departments. 'I see Ken from Marketing got the Supremo's job,' is more likely to be the harbinger of a successful reign than, 'Oh, Christ! It looks as if we're going to be working for that stuck-up swine Smyth-Jones.' Often, if winners have contact with other firms in the course of their work, their network will have expanded to include secretaries, shop-floor workers and executives in any number of firms. This not only helps their performance in their current job but is a useful source of intelligence and of possible 'parachutes'. Winners keep moving out from their bases, gaining in confidence and winning friends as they go, so that whatever happens, whatever they need, and perhaps more importantly, whatever anyone else may need, they always know someone they can phone.

THE DIRTY RASCAL SYNDROME

There are a lot of advantages to building up comfort zones – so many in fact that many managements have latched on to the idea and are making whole companies and huge organisations into surrogate families. Such firms usually begin by making it clear when they plan their recruiting campaigns that they are looking for winners, either by headhunting the top people from universities or by advertising for recruits with slightly higher qualifications than those required by similar companies.

Their application forms are usually long and detailed while the interviews – there are often several of them – are probing and, even for quite junior positions, are undertaken by obviously senior staff. The applicant is left with the impression that, if he or she is lucky enough to get the job, they will be joining a company which is already looking for high flyers.

This impression is confirmed by salaries higher, if only slightly, than the norm and by well thought-out training and welfare schemes and incentive plans and frequent career reviews. There is also usually a team-based departmental structure in which all the department heads are trained, sympathetic, winning leaders most of whom have started their careers with the company in question.

This is great. Such firms are evident winners and we have to approve of their methods as they embody many of our winning attitudes and strategies. They begin by boosting the successful candidate's self-worth and go on to provide cash incentives, job satisfaction and a series of comfort-zone bases, all fitting together like a Russian doll and lasting, if not from the cradle to the grave, from first pay packet to pension.

Unfortunately, there is a potential downside if self-worth and team spirit lead to elitism and the feeling that those who work for the company are splendid and winning human beings while those outside the company are at best losers and at worst *Untermenschen* or sub-humans.

EVERYBODY CAN BE A WINNER

True winners know that just as they themselves are miracles every other human being is a miracle too and should be regarded as such, although this does not mean that there aren't some people around who appear to be irredeemable rats or total deadlegs. It does mean that winners look for the best even in members of the Jobsworth clan and try to help them to become winners.

Winning couples and winning families know they have a good thing going but this shouldn't lead to them excluding other couples or families.

In the same way, potentially winning departments, firms and, for that matter, countries should guard against elitism. Dividing the world into 'them and us' is fine provided we don't condemn 'them' as barbarians or 'lesser breeds beyond the pale'. Pride is fine; elitism is not, and racism and nationalism – not patriotism – are 'the last refuge of the scoundrel'.

Holistic winning involves being winners in every sphere of life ourselves and the realisation that the more people who win the more everybody wins.

Tips from the Top

Customers who complain are your best customers.

Time is the number one competitor.

Always be prepared to learn from others.

Only the brave make mistakes.

When life gives you a lemon – make lemonade.

12

PLANNING TO WIN

Winners plan to win. Holistic winners plan to win in all departments of their lives, while helping other people to chalk up wins to create a winning social and working environment.

It's a big order, but fortunately we don't have to set out to change the world. Making ourselves total winners is quite sufficient, because doing so sends out waves of winning like ripples on a pool.

We don't even have to change ourselves all at once because, as we've seen, many a mickle win makes a muckle win and, eventually, winning itself becomes a habit. What we do need to do is to set out personal goals, decide what it is we need to make us into true holistic winners, and then *begin winning*.

CONFESSION TIME

Winners need a plan – in fact they need lots of plans – but most people are content to drift in some departments of their lives and there is someone we know, not a million miles away from this word processor, who has done more drifting than a message in a bottle and has only recently come to recognise the virtues of planning.

At the same time, while accepting that, for instance, an unplanned four years living on a lotus diet in the South of France may not be the greatest of career moves, we have also seen how obsessional planners often end up as over-stressed losers, especially if their plans don't work out.

The winning strategy is to make a plan and stick to it – but only as long as it proves to be viable – and to have a 'parachute' plan, or plans, in reserve, just in case.

A PLAN IS JUST A PLAN

A plan is only a plan, just as a list is merely a list, and neither has the force of a heavenly edict. Both have exactly the importance that we decide to give them and there is nothing wrong with making them an important factor in our lives, providing that we remember that they are not sacrosanct. They are *our* plans and it is up to us to change them if we wish to – or have to.

WINNING IS AN 'ALL RANKS' AFFAIR

Plans can be divided into two main categories – strategic and tactical – and in the battle to become a holistic winner each of us is his or her own general, a situation which is rendered a little more complicated by the fact that we very often have to be our junior officers and other ranks into the bargain, and are responsible not only for strategy but also for tactics, for making plans and for executing them.

Naturally, we can enlist help with our planning – from

parents, teachers, colleagues and so on, but in the end the decisions and the carrying out of them are our responsibility.

The trouble is that we often have to make long-term strategic decisions at the wrong time, long before we know all the facts – often when we are quite young – and this not only means that we may easily make the wrong decisions, but that we may be lead to give undue weight to the opinions of those who assume that they know what is best for us.

The important thing for winners to realise is that even strategic aims – perhaps especially strategic aims – are not immutable – so that if you have been talked into or forced into a path which subsequently turns out to be wrong for you, *you can and should change it.*

This is not to say that, if you or your teachers decide that your long-term strategic career aim is to become a concert violinist, you shouldn't give it your best shot. It *does* mean, however, that if you discover that you have taken the wrong route and would rather become an airline pilot, or run a business, you should change course, if possible, because *while changing horse in midstream may be difficult it's a damned sight better than drowning, along with a mount that turns out to be a non-swimmer.*

Winners begin preparing parachute plans at an early age and go on making such plans until they are absolutely certain that they are on the right track.

SO YOU WANT TO BE RICH AND FAMOUS

Do you really want to be rich and famous? There's nothing wrong with it as a strategic aim but, unless you are abso-

Winners begin planning early

lutely certain that money can buy happiness and every-thing else, it can't be the sole aim of a holistic winner because holistic winning means winning in all departments.

Almost everyone wants to be a winner in every aspect of their lives but as none of us is exactly the same as any other person, even holistic winners may elect to devote more time and energy to winning in one department than another. The trick is to achieve the balance which will make *you* a winner while making the people with whom you come into contact winners as well.

DECISION TIME

Deciding on our strategic and tactical aims is difficult but the decisions are not immutable and, in fact, if we didn't change our minds at some stage it would mean that we had learned nothing – which would place us firmly among the losers.

With this in mind, we can now put down on paper our long-term strategic aims, rating each aspect of our lives in accordance with its – current – importance. Remember – we are planning for perfection even if we do have to settle for a little less.

Set down all your long-term winning aims, awarding points out of a hundred for importance. The categories might be, for example:

WEALTH

HEALTH

ATTRACTIVE APPEARANCE

POWER AND INFLUENCE

A HAPPY FAMILY LIFE
CAREER SUCCESS
HAPPY CHILDREN
SUCCESSFUL CHILDREN
A RESPECTED PLACE IN THE COMMUNITY
FAME

Ideally, perhaps we should have awarded ten importance points to each category, but in practice we have almost certainly split our list into two areas of importance and awarded more importance points to one area than the other so that we may, for instance, be over-emphasising Wealth, Power, Career Success, Fame and a Respected Place in the Community at the expense of the others or vice versa.

Holistic winning implies that winning in one area will help us achieve wins in other areas so, instead of awarding each category a number of importance points, let's regard each one as a building block with which we can build an extremely stable structure like a pyramid.

This might yield something like:

FAME

WEALTH, POWER

CAREER SUCCESS, SUCCESSFUL CHILDREN, RESPECTED PLACE

HEALTH, ATTRACTIVE APPEARANCE, HAPPY FAMILY LIFE, HAPPY CHILDREN

Now add in any extra strategic aims you may have thought of like Leisure or Cultural Development and build your own holistic winner's pyramid. You'll see that there are different ways of building your pyramid depending mainly on what you choose as the apex – but not so many as you might think.

You could try including some specifics in your building blocks, indicating that you want to be, for instance, a famous politician or a famous ballet dancer or that 'health' in your case depends to some extent on losing a couple of stone.

In most cases, deciding to become, say, a famous ballet dancer is meaningless without the lower steps of the pyramid. This doesn't mean that such a decision is fatuous in itself but merely that it should go into another category of 'overall' strategic decisions.

PLAN NUMBER ONE – THE ULTIMATE DREAM

Winners must have a dream because, although they may not be convinced that it really is better to 'travel hopefully' than to arrive, they know that in the long run it is hope that makes the journey bearable and can also make it fun.

Let's by all means dream about the super win that projects us into the International Household Name class, provided we remember that there is – or should be – only one heavyweight champion of the world and relatively few great painters, presidents or multi-millionaires.

Deciding from the beginning that we will derive no satisfaction from anything less than becoming the Champ, the Numero Uno or the wealthiest person in the world is the way to obsession. It may or may not make the realisation of any particular dream more likely but, by depriving us of the enjoyment of a myriad small and medium-sized wins along the way, it stands a very good chance of turning the dream into a nightmare.

Most of those who decide that only the ultimate goal is worthwhile must learn to live with the deadly poison of other people's success, while their own successes, however numerous, seem bitter and unsatisfying simply because they fall short of the ultimate triumph.

Holistic winners do have an ultimate goal – or goals – but they are able to visualise their lives – past, present and future – as a whole, and they know there are opportunities for all of us to win hundreds of victories and that we should appreciate and celebrate them all.

PLAN NUMBER TWO – THE ACHIEVABLE DREAM

Perhaps your ultimate dream is to become an immortal literary figure and to take your place in the Pantheon alongside Shakespeare, Goethe, Dante and the rest. Why not? It's the sort of dream you can enjoy dreaming every now and again and it gives you a finite goal.

Let's face it, though, not every writer is going to be read and quoted a thousand years from now and it would be a shame if the thought that you might not be among the few were to spoil your enjoyment of writing – or of your life.

Writing a best-seller, a prize-winning book or both, is probably the best achievable dream a writer can reasonably hope for and, rather like drawing a horse in the Irish Sweepstake, it brings with it a chance to win the ultimate prize, even though the odds may range from a million to one to odds on.

PLAN NUMBER THREE – TACTICAL DREAMING

It's obvious – even though some people who dream of being writers don't seem to appreciate it – that the first and essential step in becoming the author of a best-selling book is *to write a book* and usually it helps to make it the best you are capable of writing. Then the book has to be brought to the attention of a publisher, who in turn has to submit it to the judgement of critics and the public. To reach the public the writer must plan to submit the book himself, attempt to interest an agent, or have it printed privately and tour the country on horseback with book-filled saddle bags, like Billy Holt, the author of the minor classic *I Haven't Unpacked*.

PLAN NUMBER FOUR – PRACTICAL DREAMING

Equally obvious – and equally incomprehensible to many people – is the fact that in order to write a book you have to put your bottom firmly on a seat in front of a typewriter and stay there with suitable breaks for wine, tea or whatever turns you on until several hundred pages of blank paper are covered with your golden words.

As with most things, the best way to begin is to start. We can always change or even throw away what we have written.

PLAN NUMBER FIVE – PREPLANNING THE DREAM

Most people have to earn a living while dreaming of immortality, in addition to which they usually have to gain some knowledge and/or experience before they begin.

This is an important planning stage which could involve specialist education, a relevant associated occupation like journalism or a completely different specialist occupation which would yield memories or notebooks filled with usable plots, situations and characters.

PLAN NUMBER SIX – THE ULTIMATE DREAM

A bit of a cheat this, since Plan Number One was the Ultimate Dream but let's go back to the Irish Sweepstake. Naturally you can't win without a ticket, but what makes you buy it? Usually the dream, however vague, that you might become the ultimate winner. Then you have to find the cash for a ticket, draw a horse and finally win the ultimate prize. The dream is no use without the ticket and the ticket is of little use without the dream.

Of course, the sort of planning we've been talking about doesn't apply merely to writing a book destined to become a classic. Much the same thing applies if our ultimate aim is to become a billionaire or a painter who will rank among the Masters.

In the winning scheme of things, the ultimate dream comes first – and last.

PLANNING FOR IMPORTANCE AND EMPHASIS

Never leave an analogy while it still has a breath of life in it, we say, so we'll stick with the Irish Sweepstake in which there are several very important decisions to be made on the way to the realisation of that ultimate dream, most of them concerned with how much importance we are prepared to give the possibility of achieving the ultimate dream at any given time. How important is the big win and how much are we prepared to expend on it, given our other important objectives?

In this instance, we must first decide to invest in a ticket or not, then decide whether we want a whole ticket or a share, and then, if we draw a horse, decide whether we wish to sell the ticket – favourite or outsider -- for what is usually a considerable sum, or go for broke and the ultimate dream.

In the case of other ultimate dreams, similar decisions have to be made about the investment of time, effort or, in some cases, money, from the time we dream our first ultimate dream.

The important difference is that holistic winning, as opposed to gambling, is not an either/or situation because, as we have seen, a win in one sector, far from depriving another important sector, usually nourishes it, helping us to become total winners.

TACTICAL PLANNING

Tactical planning, because of its short-term application, is less subject to major change than strategic planning, but here again, rigidity is for losers. Winners should always be prepared to change their tactics, especially when confronted by an unlooked-for problem, which losers call bad luck, or by an unexpected opportunity – which the same people refer to as good luck – implying that such examples of good fortune are somehow reserved for winners.

One of the most important things about tactical plans is that they should be achievable, and achievable within a specific time-span. Aim, for instance, to *double* your income in five years' time, not just 'to make more money'.

Tactical planning is best carried out in stages; set your objectives, estimate stages, move to stage one, dig in, recce, move to stage two, dig in, recce, move on and so on. Of course, no one is suggesting that winners must have infantry training but the military have recently perfected the art of moving forward with comparative safety in dangerous territory, so perhaps we can learn from them.

A WINNER'S DIARY

Five years is about the limit for a tactical plan – after all, no one even knows with certainty what will happen to them tomorrow – and it divides neatly into manageable yearly segments, so set a five-year plan which will fit your overall strategic aims.

Then take your diary and mark out your short-term and long-term aims in all departments of your life in red. Fill in your diary in the ordinary way in blue as you go along and every so often compare the two, writing down in a third colour why you think you achieved your aims or where you think you may have gone wrong.

Indicate where a win in one department of your life has helped you to become more of a winner in others. Indicate also the ways in which you have sloughed off 'work' at home or in the workplace, either by becoming more efficient or by taking a new view of what was essential.

Use another two-colour system to plan your week and summarise your achievements at the end of each month.

Don't forget – *a plan is a tool, not a rule.* After all, they are all *your* plans and that makes you the boss.

USE YOUR KNOW-WHERE

Everyone accepts the importance of know-how but in these days know-where is even more essential.

Know-where is simply the ability to lay your hands on information and people as and when required and it is a paramount weapon in the winner's armoury, both in the short term and the long term.

Winners never say 'I don't know' if they are unable to give an immediate answer, but always, 'I don't know right now but I can let you have the information by such and such a time or day at the latest.'

Winners on the home front, for example, know where they can find at short notice a qualified plumber, electrician, garage man and the rest. They also have numbers for solicitors, doctors, insurance companies and so on who have been recommended over the years and put on the list of important numbers – together with the name of the person who recommended them – even if there is no need for their services at the moment.

One way to make sure that your list of emergency numbers is adequate is to spend a few minutes playing the Worst Possible Scenario game in which you imagine the most awful series of disasters and find out if you have all the contacts you need.

PLANNING TO KNOW

What you have done in this domestic context is to plan to know in advance where to find the information you may need and you can use this Worst Possible Scenario method in many other branches of your life. 'Who would I ring', for example, 'if my job became untenable?' might be one question.

Fortunately, while your know-where is useful in cases of disaster, it is absolutely essential to the preparation and implementation of your winning plans.

Plan not so much to know everything you are going to need to know but to know-where to find what you will need to know.

Identify your sources of information in advance. You do not need to carry masses of information in your head – you *do* need to know exactly where to find it.

In much the same way, you don't really need know-how. What you need is to know-where to find someone with know-how, either within your company or outside it.

It is useful and agreeable to have some specialised know-how and winners recognise the value of this as a morale booster. However, a person who has the know-where to lay hands on, say fifty people with know-how is likely to be a winner.

In practice, winners like to have a certain amount of know-how and at the same time to know-where to find the people whose know-how they need at the moment and those whose expertise will be useful to them in the future.

PLANNING FOR MIRACLES

Winners can forget everything they have been told about 'not expecting the earth' because winners know that they are entitled to have high hopes – in fact, as we pointed out, every one of us is a miracle and winners are merely the ones who recognise the fact.

Winners know that a high level of self-worth leads to high expectations and that, just as the value placed on us by others is governed by the value we place on ourselves, what we receive in life is largely governed by our expectations.

To put it in purely material terms, if our ambition in life is to make £10,000 a year, few people are likely to offer us more. On the other hand, if we expect to make £100,000, they may well talk us into accepting, say, £65,000 and perks.

In the same way, if we expect our partnership to be a happy and successful one and plan to make our expectations come true, we stand a better chance than those who anticipate the worst.

So let's not just plan to be winners – let's make plans to become super-winners in every department of life – and start winning today.

Also by Nick Thornely and Dan Lees . . .

HOW TO BE A WINNER

Most of us want to be winners – which isn't too surprising as 'winners tend to be happier and more exciting than other people and, while they may or not be richer, their lives have a sparkle that losers can never experience'. Are you a winner? People in top jobs sound as if they should be winners but although presidents and monarchs hold the world's top jobs some of them have definitely not been winners.

How to be a Winner shows how to identify the real winners: the winning president, the winning executive, the winning secretary or the winning doorman. It will also help you spot a winning company, a winning team or a winning country. Nick Thornely and Dan Lees – both winners in their very different ways – maintain that in the game of life, as opposed to sporting contests, everyone can be a winner and that a winning company, for example, should be staffed by winners from the newest recruit up to the chairman. Enjoyment, they maintain, is the key factor in developing the winning habit. If you are ambitious, enjoying what you do could take you right to where you can do the most good for yourself and your company while stress is strictly for losers.

This amusing and thought-provoking look at the way we live and work will annoy the 'more than my job's worth' employee and the 'you're not here to think' type of employer, but the rest of us may well find that being a winner is more important than we realised. Winning – and helping other people to win – is what life is all about, all of which makes it essential to know *how to be a winner*.

'Packed with confidence-boosting ideas' . . . **Executive Development**

Published by Mercury Books
£6.99 (paperback)   ISBN 1–85252–059–0